Chip E. Miller
Pacific Lutheran University

Instructor's Manual to Accompany

Marketing

Research

Exercises

WEST PUBLISHING COMPANY
MINNEAPOLIS/ST. PAUL   NEW YORK   LOS ANGELES   SAN FRANCISCO

WEST'S COMMITMENT TO THE ENVIRONMENT

In 1906, West Publishing Company began recycling materials left over from the production of books. This began a tradition of efficient and responsible use of resources. Today, up to 95% of our legal books and 70% of our college texts and school texts are printed on recycled, acid-free stock. West also recycles nearly 22 million pounds of scrap paper annually—the equivalent of 181,717 trees. Since the 1960s, West has devised ways to capture and recycle waste inks, solvents, oils, and vapors created in the printing process. We also recycle plastics of all kinds, wood, glass, corrugated cardboard, and batteries, and have eliminated the use of Styrofoam book packaging. We at West are proud of the longevity and the scope of our commitment to the environment.

Production, Prepress, Printing and Binding by West Publishing Company.

 TEXT IS PRINTED ON 10% POST CONSUMER RECYCLED PAPER    PRINTED WITH SOY INK™   ∞

COPYRIGHT © 1995 by   WEST PUBLISHING CO.
610 Opperman Drive
P.O. Box 64526
St. Paul, MN 55164–0526

ISBN 0–314–05926–1

CONTENTS

MARKET RESEARCH EXERCISES

Introduction

It is suggested that the students have their assignments spread out evenly over the course of the term even though some of them are pertinent to specific chapters. This avoids queuing up for library resources. Also, it is a good idea to assign each student a separate industry from the list at the beginning of this workbook. Choosing an industry for them usually results in their learning about something they had no previous knowledge of. Such random selection also prevents them from passing on their information to friends or members of their social groups that might take the class in succeeding terms.

The material on secondary data sources tends to create lines at the library. If you choose to do so, you may provide open-ended deadlines for the submission of these assignments. This is particularly true in the case of such works at <u>The Encyclopedia of Associations</u> or the <u>Commercial Atlas and Marketing Guide</u>, where only one volume may be found in the library.

These exercises are meant to serve three primary purposes. The first is to expose the student to materials that are available as secondary data sources for decision making by marketing managers. The second is to have them work with simple examples of standard market research techniques to better understand how they work, where they are inappropriate for use, and how to interpret the information gathered using them. Finally, the manual hopes to have the students refresh their skills in statistics and, perhaps, regression, so that they do not forget how these important tools are employed.

Before the students embark on secondary data hunts, it is important that the professor inform the librarian in advance that the students are coming so that the library can be prepared. If time permits, a class spent with the librarian as teacher is a very valuable experience. It is also a good idea to locate in advance which sources can be had in which libraries before assignments are made. Again, the librarian can be a valuable aid in answering this question. This probably seems obvious, but the author has been tripped up before. Sometimes the public library has resources that the school does not, and vice versa. A bit of searching in advance will greatly reduce grousing on the part of the students if something apparently cannot be found.

Although most of the secondary data exercises are centered on specific volumes in the library, there is a set of questions for international marketing research that are "free form". These simple international business exercises prescribe no specific texts, allowing students the "luxury" of learning about the library and giving the reference librarian a chance to show his/her skills. The professor may wish to check the sources the students reference, since there are multiple correct answers for this exercise and some of them may not be noted in this manual.

The following is a list of industries for use by students in their research during the term. Should the instructor wish to do so, other options are available from Simmons data or Predicasts.

cigarettes	fishing equipment
housewares	discount stores
sports cars	lighting
motorcycles	armaments
shoes	department stores
batteries	games
robots	bicycles
toys	insurance
amusement parks	lasers
pest control	calculators
TV sets	photographic film
personal computers	watches
razors	jewelry
cameras	pets
eyewear	beer
restaurants	greeting cards
explosives	hotels & motels
soft drinks	helicopters
diesel engines	business magazines
furniture	recreational vehicles

Module 1

MARKETING RESEARCH IN MANAGEMENT DECISION MAKING

ASSIGNMENT 1

Management Problem #1

You have been approached by an entrepreneur who has an idea for a new rocking chair. The chair has a mechanical back-massaging apparatus, is made of solid oak and is handmade by an American craftsman. The designer has sold them for two years at home shows and in nearby towns and even has a letter from the President of the United States praising his chair. He is interested in having the chairs mass produced so that he can expand distribution nationally.

Current wholesale prices for a finished chair are $250. Retail prices are $375-$450 depending on the exact configuration chosen. Preliminary talks with a furniture manufacturer in Washington indicate costs would run $285 instead of the $125 the entrepreneur has calculated is his cost to build one. Your business partner, who has some experience in retail furniture sales, says he talked to a buyer from a large department store chain who is interested in the chair.

What other information would you need before agreeing to invest $50,000 in this venture?

Discussion outline:

Have other chairs been tried and failed? No.

Does the designer have a patent? No. It may not be important because he does not have the funds to fight a copyright/patent battle if someone did copy his design.

How to market--stores, catalogs, home parties? Students may suggest this, but they are getting ahead of themselves. They haven't established that there is a concentrated demand for the product, how big it is or where it is. Even if the demand exists, they don't know if it is possible to reach it for the price that it demands.

Current competition--There is a massaging recliner that is electric that is made by a Japanese company that sells for approximately $1500. It is available from Sharper Image and a Japanese department store. It is upholstered and quite sophisticated compared to what you have to sell.

Demand for such a product--The fact that some sales were made indicate there is some demand, but how much and whether it can be reached profitably are open to question. No segmentation studies have been done, although clues exist.

Market segment--how concentrated? who are they?

Sales volume--exactly how many chairs has he sold, and over what time period? How were they sold?

Customers sold to--how many were they, what characteristics did they have.

Retailers' reaction--this is the crux of the problem. In reality, manufacturer's agents said the chair was ugly, that it was far too expensive compared to other rockers (regardless of the fact that they did not massage one's back pains away), and that they would not carry it. When we spoke to retailers, they were not interested in having it on their showroom floors. In essence, we could not get any exposure for the product through normal channels.

Cost to manufacture--why is there such a disparity between the entrepreneur's manufacturing cost and the Washington cost? Can it be reduced? Or is there a need to have them produced in Washington at all? Perhaps the demand is small enough that the limited capacity of the entrepreneur is sufficient for the time being.

Need for a full run instead of a prototype--why would you produce a full run of chairs at this point? You don't know if they will sell. It would be foolish to begin manufacturing before the bugs are eliminated from the prototype.

Previous attempts at selling through channels. The entrepreneur tried to work with Sears previously, but Sears wanted very high volumes at a very low price, so the deal fell through.

Can we make it cheaper? This is really irrelevant if other crucial factors fail (e.g. channel members won't accept the product), but someone will mention it.

Students should have field day with this situation, as it is obvious that not enough information has been collected to seriously consider doing anything with this venture yet. A list of items to consider is as follows:

1. What sort of volume has this entrepreneur generated in the last 2 years? The fact that he has been able to support himself in some fashion from these chairs does not necessarily indicate that national demand exists. He is, after all, a solo operation with a few subcontractors. Is the region he lives in different from the rest of the nation? (The person in question is from Montana and the chairs were sold largely in Montana, Idaho and Oregon, with one retail store in Colorado carrying them. The latter usually ordered only one at a time because they did not move quickly.)

2. When were these chairs sold? Was demand spread evenly across the year or was it seasonal? The investors were looking to bring the chair to market for Christmas in the hope that it might be successful initially as a novelty item.

3. What type of customer bought these chairs? Individuals or institutions or stores? What type of stores? The demographics of the customer are missing. As it turned out, pregnant mothers liked them, as did people with back problems. A few hospital maternity wards had them and expressed pleasure with the chairs, but only bought one or two for the ward. No mothers purchased one for their use at home after they were discharged. As for back pain sufferers, think about the daunting task of identifying concentrations of these people.

The idea of selling to medical supply houses was raised but none had bought them to this point. Also, as mentioned, only a couple of small furniture stores had the chairs in stock. Virtually the entire volume was moved through home shows and county fairs.

4. Who really is our target market?

Students may feel that they should go out and survey the general public to see what the demand is. It is suggested that they first approach those members of the distribution channel who will control access to the chair. Talking to a manufacturer's rep about carrying the chair will give immediate feedback about its chances for success and dramatically limits the size of the survey needed. Another easy step would be to talk to furniture retailers in a major city and ask them what their thoughts are. Granted, if the results from a marketing survey of potential buyers were positive, it would be a useful bit of sales information to influence retailers. However, if they are not enthusiastic about the product, customer survey results may not be enough to persuade them.

As it turned out, the manufacturer's reps universally decried the product as unattractive, far too expensive in its present configuration, and a specialty item. It would not double as a regular rocking chair but was really only useful as something to massage one's back.

A specialty item? Someone may ask about Sharper Image. That deserves a look, given the unique nature of the product. (It was turned down as not compatible with their line of products--too rustic.)

ASSIGNMENT 2

Management Problem #2

You are doing research for a company that wishes to import glassware from China for sale in the United States. It is important that your supplier is reliable, meets your price guidelines, and that problems can be rectified quickly when they arise. Your field agent, who is a native Chinese, suggests that Shanghai is a good place to focus because it has a large, modern port and a number of glassware manufacturers in the area. What information should you obtain before selecting a supplier?

Discussion:

The following issues should arise in the discussion or should be raised in some fashion by the instructor.

Telephone access to suppliers.

This is a common problem in many countries, especially LDCs. Even some European nations suffer from year long waits and abysmal service even after installation. Here, suppliers out of the city do not have telephones.

Price lists.

These are essential if you are to act as a broker for a manufacturer. Without them, you cannot begin to negotiate with wholesalers and retailers in the U.S. to sell your product, nor can you tell what your profit margins might be for given items. However, almost none of the manufacturers will give you price lists showing their wholesale prices--they will only quote you on a per-order basis.

Samples and up-to-date catalogs.

The catalogs available are full of products that they no longer manufacture and the samples often do not reflect the overall quality of a standard production run. They may be better or worse, or may be items that are no longer manufactured but are sent as samples because they happen to be available.

Returns or incorrect orders.

Your potential suppliers will not accept returns readily. To offset this, you would need to keep large inventories available in the U.S. so that you could deal with the retailer's problem at once, then settle with your Chinese supplier later.

Module 2

THE MARKETING RESEARCH PROCESS

The most important step in the research process is the identification of an opportunity or problem. Until this step is carefully carried out, one should not proceed. The following vignettes represent situations where there apparently is an opportunity that should be pursued. The question put to the student is, has the process been carried out correctly or is further investigation warranted?

Students should judge the research presented on the following points: accuracy, currency, sufficiency, availability and relevance.

ASSIGNMENT 3

Situation #1

One of your research associates lives in Seattle and has two teenage children, one male and one female. The son's birthday was in October and he asked for boxer shorts. A query indicates that his classmates also think that they are the latest rage. Trim fitting is out, baggy is in. Even his daughter is expressing some interest in them as everyday wear or loungewear. The researcher believes that a major ad campaign is in order so that your company can hit the Christmas market with these items and make a killing in the youth market, especially young women who are more style conscious and more extensive clothing buyers, rather than selling them to older men.

Discussion, situation #1:

The following questions should be raised by the students or the professor.

You got the information in October, and he wants to hit the Christmas market. But all the stores have already ordered in June--an ad campaign now is not feasible. Prepping for next Christmas may be argued for, but you have no idea if this is a clothing fad or a trend.

How big is the sample? Is it random?

Does the region reflect any peculiarities? Seattle is hardly Kansas City or Lincoln in terms of taste. Or does the youth market represent a homogeneous one across the country?

What survey instrument was used? It sounds as if the questions may have been leading or inadequate to determine anything useful in terms of level of interest.

How accurate were the responses? How thorough were they? Can this data be replicated on demand?

Is there any indication that someone else has already tried the same idea? Nothing in the case suggested that a competitive analysis had been done.

ASSIGNMENT 4

Situation #2

You have a close friend who is a Filipino who brought a new board game to your house for a party. This game proved to be a hit with the professionals you had at the party, who found the strategy and challenge more interesting than RISK and less difficult and absorbing than chess. The game is unknown in the U.S. but you believe that it would be a success because "thinking games" are always popular. Also, you read an article in MARKETING NEWS indicating that a new chain of adult toy stores is flourishing and you believe it would be the ideal outlet for such a game.

Discussion, situation #2:

The fact that the game is foreign may be a hindrance. There are distribution questions to be answered as well as the issue of copyrights. It may well be that you can legally copy the work and not have to go through a Filipino manufacturer.

How well is RISK doing these days? Are any other new strategy games on the market at this point? What has their introduction been like? What are the general trends in adult toys at present?

Your sample is a few professionals. They are not described in detail, nor is their behavior detailed in terms of the region of the country, their education or work experience. What ages are these people? There is a distinct possibility that younger people may prefer outdoor activity when their extremely busy jobs permit it. Also, what will other social classes think of the game?

Where is this article from MARKETING NEWS? Was it really pertinent to the question at hand?

Questions about sample size, randomness, and questionnaire design should be answered.

Has this person found out when the large toy shows are held? If it has been missed this year, the chances for launching the product are slim indeed.

ASSIGNMENT 5

Situation #3

Your best friend has been a herpetologist and dinosaur buff since childhood. The recent resurgence of interest in dinosaurs has sparked sales of books, models, replica fossils and other products. Your friend comes to you with the exciting news that latex models of real lizards are now for sale in World of Wonder stores. He believes that monitor lizards, which look like miniature dinosaurs, will become all the rage in the pet trade because of the dinosaur euphoria and the cast models of monitors in the stores. He has a number of contacts in the reptile trade and believes that you could get exclusive rights to distribute the soon-to-be sought after lizards.

Discussion, situation #3:

Any chance of bias here on the part of the researcher? Someone that close to the subject may be prejudiced in favor of its success. They may have a good idea of what similar people may like to see, but that group is a minority of unknown size and dispersion.

Dinosaurs are not modern day lizards, despite the similarities. No present day reptiles really come close on size and if they did, people would be wont to care for them. Making the leap from interest in dinosaurs to interest in their modern relatives may be too great.

Who is buying monitor lizards now? What restrictions are there on ownership? What ethical considerations are there in owning wild animals that will grow to considerable size and may become a burden or danger to their owners or their owner's friends and family? Many monitors are on endangered species lists and a number of the more popular species will grow to substantial size. Previous problems with caimans ("alligators") as pets surfaced when the pets outgrew the small aquaria they were sold in and were released by their owners or sent to zoos. Cruelty to the animals resulted in many cases, as well as ill-conceived legislation aimed at denying anyone the opportunity to own wild reptiles.

Can one extrapolate from sales of toys to sales of live animals?

Who is buying these toys? Adults, children, or schools that use them as science models in classrooms? How well are they selling? The fact that they have been found in a couple of stores does not imply success. For that matter, are they being distributed nationally by World of Wonder? What is the scope of that retail chain? Does any other chain carry them?

Module 3

SECONDARY DATA SOURCES

This section centers on secondary data and its use. In my experience, most students are unaware of the variety of published data sources and do not fully exploit what they do know about. Given the drive for greater efficiency in companies with tight budgets, the ability to use already published data is critical.

ASSIGNMENT 6

Literature Review of an Industry

Your instructor will have assigned to you one of the industries listed in the front of this workbook. You are expected to conduct a literature review of this industry using current periodicals. You will be limited to magazines, journals and newspapers. Attach a bibliography of your sources using the format chosen by your instructor.

Industry: _____

Write a brief history (100 words or less) of your industry.

_____

_____

_____

_____

_____

List the major competitors or top brands and their national market shares.

Competitor or Brand   **Market Share**

_____

_____

_____

What are some recent developments in the industry (e.g. new products)?

_____

_____

_____

Describe career opportunities for marketing majors in this industry.

_____

_____

_____

_____

ASSIGNMENT 7

Company Research

In this exercise, you will asked to select a single company from the industry you have been assigned and collect information about it. This exercise is tantamount to what you might do if looking for a job or seeking information about a competitor for further analysis. (It is suggested that you use the Dun & Bradstreet Million Dollar Directory or the Standard and Poor's Register to find this information.)

Name of the company: _____

Corporate address: _____

_____

Telephone: _____

President or CEO: _____

If the firm has multiple product lines, select a single one and list the other officers that are involved with it by position and name.

Position   **Name**

_____

_____

_____

_____

SECONDARY DATA SOURCES

The following is a list of the most common secondary data sources used in marketing research studies. You will be asked a series of questions pertaining to the industry that you have been assigned. Answer them completely and understandably, as if you were submitting a brief report to a marketing manager.

U.S. Industrial Outlook
Standard and Poor's Industry Surveys
Predicasts Forecasts
Predicasts F & S Index
Business Periodicals Index
Wall Street Journal Index
ABI Inform
Dun's Business Ranking
Commercial Atlas and Marketing Guide
Encyclopedia of Associations
Simmons Data
Thomas Register
Market Share Reporter
Brands and Their Companies

If there is no data for the question asked, fill in the space with NO DATA or N/A. Do not leave the question blank. The instructor otherwise has no way of knowing why you chose to omit an answer.

If your industry cannot be found in the source called for, ask you professor for a substitute.

DATA SOURCES & THEIR CONTENTS

Information	Source
industry prospects	U.S. Industrial Outlook Standard & Poor's Industry Surveys Wall Street Journal
value of goods & services	US Industrial Outlook
sales forecasts by product	Predicasts Forecasts Predicasts F & S Index
sales volume by firm	Dun & Bradstreet Million Dollar Directory Thomas Register Market Share Reporter Dun's Business Ranking
market share by firm	Market Share Reporter Dun's Business Ranking
market share by nation	Market Share Reporter F & S Index International or Europe
industry rank	Dun's Business Ranking
number of business locations & geographic location (by SIC code)	Census of Manufactures* Census of Retail Trade* Commercial Atlas and Marketing Guide
customer characteristics (e.g. income, media choices)	Simmons Data MRI data*
consumer buying power	Sales and Marketing Management Commercial Atlas and Marketing Guide
brand names: by company	Brands and Their Companies
general	Business Periodicals Index Wall Street Journal ABI Inform

* -- **not in this workbook**

products supplied:

general	ABI Inform
	Business Periodicals Index
SIC code	Standard & Poor's Industry Surveys
	Thomas Register

officers   Dun & Bradstreet Million Dollar Directory*
                                                 Standard & Poors Register*

company size (no. of employees)   Dun & Bradstreet Million Dollar Directory*
                                                 Standard & Poors Register*

affiliations   Encyclopedia of Associations

* -- not in this workbook

U.S. Industrial Outlook

This volume contains annual forecasts of the U.S. economy made by the Department of Commerce. Information is listed by SIC code. Major groups have 2 digit codes, industry groups 3 digits and industries 4 digits. Output is listed by individual factory and by industry, with much information coming from the *Census of Manufactures*. The value of goods and services is given in current dollars and constant dollars. The latter allows you to compare real changes in output over time.

You will be asked to investigate your industry and answer the following questions about its current situation and future prognosis.

Write the name of your industry here. _____

List the SIC code for your industry _____

Is your industry regulated by any federal agency? If so, what is the name of that agency and which larger government body does it belong in? (e.g. the Food and Drug Administration [FDA] is part of the Department of Agriculture)

Regulating agency _____

Overseeing department _____

_____

Summarize the current situation for this industry.

_____

_____

_____

4. Describe the short term and long term projections for your industry.

Short term: _____

_____

Long term: _____

_____

5. What is the outlook for international trade in this industry?

_____

_____

_____

6. How much was spent on research and development (R & D) in the last year in this industry?

_____

7. What significant events occurred in this industry during the last year?

_____

_____

ASSIGNMENT 8B

Standard and Poor's Industry Survey

These surveys are assembled annually, with revisions during the year for the current analyses. Both Basic and Current analyses of industries are offered. These examine the prospects of an industry, its trends and its problems. The comparative company analysis allows the reader to compare growth in sales and earnings of leading companies.

Write the name of your industry here: _____

What is the SIC code for your industry? _____

Who are the major companies and what are their ranks by sales volume?

Company   **Rank**   **Sales Volume**

_____

_____

_____

What are the major products in your industry? To whom are they important (e.g. government, other industry [name them], consumers).

Product   **Used by**

_____

_____

_____

List the important events that have happened this year in your trade line.

_____

_____

_____

Which firms in your industry figure prominently in the S&P survey? List their names here, with a brief note of why they were mentioned.

_____

_____

_____

_____

_____

_____

_____

What is the outlook for this industry both in the U.S. and abroad? Be more precise than just "good" or "bad". Describe expected breakthroughs, new trading alliances or other major events anticipated. On the foreign notes, indicate for the most important nations what the outlook is, if the data are present.

U.S. _____

_____

_____

_____

Foreign: _____

_____

_____

_____

Write an abstract of the survey (150 words or less). This should include such details as the major players, the outlook for the industry, which foreign countries figure prominently in the report and which products are in ascent or decline.

_____

_____

_____

_____

_____

Predicasts Forecasts

This data source compiles forecasts on products, markets, industry and economic aggregates for the U.S. and North America. The information is published quarterly, with a list of sources given in the index. Forecasts are grouped by 7 digit SIC code.

Give the name and the SIC code for your product:

_____

How does this SIC code differ from other uses you have seen?

This one is 7 digit, not 2 or 3 or 4.

Describe the activities for your product over a 3 year period. What pattern do you see?

_____

_____

What do B, S and L stand for?

base, short range and long range

What do f, h, k and z mean in the time period section?

fiscal year, crop year, model year and 21st century

Name 2 different sources for your forecast.

_____

_____

What annual growth is projected?

_____

ASSIGNMENT 8D

Predicasts F & S Index

This index contains company, product and industry information from over 750 business-related publications and reports. Included is information on mergers and acquisitions, new products, technology developments and socio-political factors affecting business.

The index comes in 2 volumes: the industries and products information is found in the green pages and the company information is in the white pages.

Give the 3 or 4 digit SIC code for your product._____

List the year of the index you are using. _____

Give the 7 digit SIC code and name of your product.

_____

What is happening with this product?

_____

_____

What future developments are discussed?

_____

_____

List 2 companies involved with this product.

_____

_____

Describe other events that pertain to one of these 2 companies. How will they fare based on these reports?

_____

_____

_____

Conduct the same search in either the international or European edition of this index.

Which areas does the International volume cover?

_____

_____

How does the global scene differ from the U.S.?

_____

_____

_____

Which company or country is in the lead technologically? in sales?

_____

_____

Which countries and companies are major global players?

_____

_____

ASSIGNMENT 8E

Business Periodicals Index

This index is published monthly, with an annual cumulation each August. The publication lists a wide array of articles of interest to business. These articles are given in alphabetical order, without regard to SIC or other codes. Its scope covers both academic journals and the popular press. The periodicals indexed are listed in the front of each volume.

Write the name of your industry here:

_____

What alternative titles does the index suggest that you look under in addition to marketing? (look to the **see also** list)

_____

Identify 3 articles that pertain to your topic, including one that discusses a single company in your industry. Give proper bibliographic citations for each of them below.

_____

_____

_____

_____

_____

_____

Summarize the contents of one of the articles.

_____

_____

_____

_____

_____

ASSIGNMENT 8F

Wall Street Journal Index

This index contains information from the Eastern edition of the *Wall Street Journal* in two separate sections. One deals with corporate news and the other deals with general news. The corporate news is arranged alphabetically by company or organization name. General news is alphabetical by person, product or geography. Approximately 4000 headings are used. The index comes in 8 monthly and 4 quarterly volumes. Stock tables are not included.

How are the geographic locations indexed?

country and state

What does the citation 5/18-9; 5 mean?

issue of May 1, page 9, column 5

What year WSJ did you use? _____

Write your topic name: _____

What else is your topic listed under? _____

_____

What is an important issue in your industry? Cite 2 articles dealing with it and summarize the contents of one.

_____

_____

_____

_____

Cite one article dealing with your topic in a foreign country.

_____

_____

How do these articles compare with others you have read in other publications? Do the findings support or contrast with those of other writers? How are these articles in terms of depth and timeliness?

_____

_____

_____

_____

ASSIGNMENT 8G

ABI Inform

List your product or industry here:

_____

What key word did you use first?

_____

How many cites did you get?

_____

Narrow your search parameters and rerun 2-3 iterations. Describe your changes here and how it reduced your citations.

_____

_____

What advantages does ABI give you? _____

_____

_____

What disadvantages are there? _____

_____

_____

Summarize one interesting article you found.

_____

_____

_____

Dun's Business Ranking

These annual volumes rank over 25,000 public and private businesses. One may locate information by state, SIC code, nation or size (sales volume or employee size). SIC codes are 4 digit.

What are the top 5 businesses in the United States?

Business	Sales Volume	SIC
_____	_____	_____
_____	_____	_____
_____	_____	_____
_____	_____	_____

Within the state you have been assigned, give the top 3 businesses, their rank in industry and their sales volume.

Business	Sales Volume	Rank
_____	_____	_____
_____	_____	_____
_____	_____	_____

List the top 3 businesses in your industry and their sales volume. (If your industry is not given in the book, either select another or use a 2 digit SIC code that corresponds to your original industry.)

Business   **Sales Volume**

_____

_____

_____

What are the top 3 foreign businesses or private businesses? If foreign, give the country of origin.

Business   **Foreign or Private?**

_____

_____

_____

How do the foreign/private firms compare with U.S. public firms in terms of sales volume and size?

Business   **Sales**   **Size**

_____

_____

_____

Commercial Atlas and Marketing Guide

This annual guide is broken into 6 sections--1) US and metropolitan maps 2) transportation and communication data 3) economic data 4) population data 5) state maps 6) index of statistics and places by state. There is also information on sales and population by 3 digit zip code and county sales data.

Your instructor will assign a state for you to work with.

State: _____

How many SMSAs (standard metropolitan statistical areas) are found within this state? Identify up to 3 of them.

_____

How many CMSAs (consolidated metropolitan statistical areas) are there? Identify up to 3 of them.

_____

What is the largest SMSA in this state? What is its population?

_____

Locate a trading area within your state. Is its center within the state or located in another state? Where is this center?

_____

Does your state have a corporate leader? If it does, what is its name and which industries is this firm in?

_____

ASSIGNMENT 8J

Calculating and Using a Buying Power Index

You have been hired by WalMart to assist in determining which cities it should target for its continued expansion. You are asked to rank order the cities in the target state based on their total sales potential. Your ranking will be arrived at by using the Buying Power Index (BPI) found in the annual "Survey of Buying Power" in **Sales and Marketing Management**.

Your instructor will assign you a state in which to work.

STATE _____

CITY   BPI

1. _____   _____

2. _____   _____

3. _____   _____

4. _____   _____

5. _____   _____

6. _____   _____

7. _____   _____

8. _____   _____

9. _____   _____

10. _____   _____

2. Explain what the difference in BPI among the various cities means.

_____

_____

_____

3. You are also asked to develop a special index for the top 5 cities on your list. According to the previous experience of WalMart, the three principal product categories should be weighted as follows. The weights are assigned based on proportion of corporate sales represented by each category.

Product Type	Weight
Drugs	.1
Food	.2
General Merchandise	.7

Use the worksheet below to compute your custom index. Use the rank from the previous section for the city designation below. All sales are in thousands of dollars.

		A		B		C		
City	Food ($000)	Food x Weight	General Mdse. ($000)	General Mdse. x Weight	Drugs ($000)	Drugs x Weight	Sum A+B+C	Index (A+B+C)/T
—	—	—	—	—	—	—	—	—
—	—	—	—	—	—	—	—	—
—	—	—	—	—	—	—	—	—
—	—	—	—	—	—	—	—	—
—	—	—	—	—	—	—	—	—

T = Total = _____   1.00

3. Did you discern any difference in rank order using the two different indices? What occurred? What difference would this make to a market researcher using these indices? What advice would you give them, if any?

_____

_____

_____

ASSIGNMENT 8K

Encyclopedia of Associations

This annual encyclopedia supplies details on almost 23,000 national and international nonprofit, trade and professional associations, sports, hobby groups and others. It is arranged by subject. Geographic and executive indices are available. Information supplied includes association name, address, number of members, services and publications.

Write the name of your industry here:

_____

What keyword(s) are associated with it in the encyclopedia?

_____

Write the section that your industry is located in.

_____

Select one organization dealing with your industry and provide:

Name of the organization:

_____

_____

Year founded: _____

Membership: _____

Affiliated with: _____

_____

Publications: _____

_____

Meeting schedule: _____

ASSIGNMENT 8L

Simmons Study of Media & Markets

These data are a study of media and markets. The results are from a large sample of U.S. adults and can be projected to the population over 18 in the lower 48 states. You may learn who reads what magazines and newspapers, who watches which shows on TV and who listens to what radio format. It also provides details on their income, age and education. Finally, it cross references the type of users of a product or service with the best media to reach them.

Your instructor will assign you one of the product series volumes. Select one product from the volume and answer the following questions.

Name of your product: _____

Is your product listed by males, females, or a combination? If a combination, what does it consist of? (e.g. archery is adults and males, with no separate female data)

_____

How many used or purchased your product within the last 12 months?

_____

What percent are in the highest use category? What is it?

_____

What age group has the largest number of people? (watch the number here--read the column heading)

_____

What region of the U.S. has the most participation?

_____

Which household income is most prevalent? _____

Which household size is most common? _____

Look at column A. What 3 magazines are best to advertise in based solely on reader numbers?
List them and their circulation numbers.

_____

_____

What radio format is best to reach your target audience? worst?

        Best_____Worst_____

What 2 evening TV shows would we choose based solely on viewer numbers? List the viewer
numbers for each program selected.

_____

Which magazines and TV programs would you recommend based on the content to most
efficiently reach your target audience?

Magazines (choose 2)

_____

TV programs (choose 2)

_____

Why did you select these? How do they differ from the ones chosen strictly on numbers of
viewers/readers?

_____

_____

ASSIGNMENT 8M

Thomas Register

This annual publication comes in 3 sections with multiple volumes--product and service, company profile, and catalogs. The company section lists assets, company executives and office locations. The catalog section includes reproductions of company catalogs. Products and services are listed alphabetically and use the modified noun system (e.g. motors: electric). Volume 17 uses a normal alphabetical index.

Your industry here: _____

What is the largest firm to supply you? _____

_____

How can you tell? _____

_____

What is the firm's rating?   In which volume did you find this information?

_____

Does this firm have a display ad? If so, please attach a copy and critique the ad. If not, what would you recommend it look like?

_____

_____

_____

What trademarks and brand names does this firm use? Where did you find this information?

_____

_____

Give the city and state of the closest branch office of this firm. Which volume was this in?

_____

_____

ASSIGNMENT 8N

Market Share Reporter

This volume is a compilation of market share reports from business periodical literature and brokerage reports. It is limited to published market shares, so the results are not exhaustive. It is broken down by corporate market share, institution, brand share and product share. Product share is subdivided by components (e.g. refrigerators, ranges, dishwashers). Both 2 digit and 4 digit SIC codes are used. Information is available on more than 5200 companies, 1700 brands and 2700 products or services.

List your SIC code and area of interest:

_____

What types of product are discussed here? List them.

_____

Report the sales by brand as shown.

Brand   **Sales**

_____

_____

_____

_____

What are the leading firms in your industry and their respective ranks?

_____

_____

_____

_____

List one more fact that you found interesting and why it was so.

_____

_____

_____

_____

Brands and Their Companies

This publication is especially useful for trade name searches. It lists over 282,000 brands from 51,000 manufacturers and distributors. Brands are listed alphabetically, with companies in a separate section. Over 120 industry-specific sources are cited. Both public and private firms are listed.

Write the name of your industry here:

_____

What are the brand names used by the top 3 firms in your industry? List only those brand names for the products in your area. Do not include brand names for subsidiaries or divisions.. (For example, Pepsico owns Frito-Lay. You should only list soft drink brands of Pepsi, not Frito products.)

Firm name #1 _____

rand names _____
nd their
products _____

_____

Firm name #2 _____

Brand names _____
and their
products _____

_____

Firm name #3 _____

Brand names _____
and their
products _____

_____

_____

What similarities do you notice between the brand names, if any?

_____

_____

_____

_____

Now look at one of the less prominent firms in your industry.

Firm name #4 _____

Brand names _____
and their
products

_____

_____

How do the brand names for its products differ from those of the leaders?

_____

_____

_____

_____

ASSIGNMENT 8P

International Business Exercises

With the increasing importance of international trade, one should also become familiar with secondary data sources that supply information for countries other than the U.S. Be sure that you write down the name of the publication you used and the year. If business reference does not have what you are looking for, check government documents.

1. Locate the leading export item from Panama.

2. Find the SIC number for Motor Vehicle Bodies. What is it? Does the U.S. have any subsidiaries in Brazil with this SIC number? List one.

3. What is the address of the Toyota subsidiary, Toyota Tsusho America Inc., located in the U.S.?

4. In September of 1988, a newspaper article discussed the Japanese stock decline resulting from Hirohito's failing health. Name the newspaper and give the exact date of the article.

5. List a Japanese company that might want to import logs from the U.S. to Japan. Give the full address and list the chief executive officer.

6. Poland is interested in doing business with the U.S. Suppose that you wanted to advertise in the largest circulation daily paper in Warsaw. What is its name and circulation figure?

7. Pratt and Whitney Aircraft has operations in other countries. In September of 1988 it announced plans to extend its engine support facility located in what country? Give the citation for the magazine or newspaper that reported this item.

Module 4

USING THE CENSUS

ASSIGNMENT 9

Store Site Selection

The data collected by the Bureau of the Census are vast and extremely useful for many purposes. This exercise will introduce you to that database.

Your instructor will assign you an SMSA to work with. You will need to search the General Characteristics of the Population and Income Characteristics of the Population tables to complete this exercise.

You have been contacted by a sporting goods store to determine a site for its new store. Past research has indicated that their target population has the following characteristics:

25 to 34 years old

income between $25,000 and $34,999

children under age 18

sing the worksheet that follows, identify those census tracts that look like the most promising areas to open the new store. Be explicit about why you chose the tracts that you did--tell the management team exactly what criteria you used to determine what areas were most suitable.

Discussion:

It is important when doing this assignment that the instructions are explicit as to what the selection criteria are for target market choice. If criteria are not prescribed, then be certain that the students are required to describe what criteria they used. Otherwise, communication breaks down if the professor ascribes one set of selection criteria as the "right" answer and students use another.

Furthermore, the professor should point out the pitfall of assuming that because the percentage of target families in a tract is high, it is a good candidate for location. If the absolute number of potential customers is low, the location is poor, despite the fact that the concentration is high. I have found it better to not tell students that in advance, but rather let it arise in class discussion or show up as a test question (perhaps as a bonus question that is mandatory to answer but not punished if answered incorrectly).

Census Tract No.	Census Tract Population		Person 25 - 34				Person $15,000-$24,999 Income		Families in Census Tract			Targeting			Summary
	No.	Total	Percent	Male	Female	Total	Percent	Total	Percent	Total	Number with Children Under 18	Percent with Children Under 18	Check If Meet Age Criterion	Check If Meets Income Criterion	Check If Meets Children Criterion	Would You Recommend As a Target Tract

Module 5

DESCRIPTIVE RESEARCH

What does 220 mean to you?

Most of you assume that means weight, and that weight is in pounds. But a 220 could be an engine size in either cubic inches (for a car) or cubic centimeters (for a motorcycle). It is also the caliber for a rifle and voltage in Europe and Asia.

The important point is, be sure you know what you are listening to and know what the units of measurement are.

What is she, a 20 footer?

This might mean either a boat or a python, depending on who is talking.

What's a 10?
1) a beautiful woman
2) a top score in gymnastics
3) a pistol caliber

38-23-36 is...

a locker combination

Your parameters for a market segment are as follows:

male, 25-40
enjoys outdoors
social club member
frequent traveler
believes clothes make the man

What do you envision as your customer?

Enclosed is a copy of a Gilmore research ad that can be used as an overhead to illustrate the problems inherent in only using descriptives.

OBSERVATION RESEARCH

This section deals with observation research, another area that, like descriptive research, is often given inadequate attention. The proposed exercises present students with 2 situations. The first gives them a wealth of data about 2 individuals and they are asked to predict what products these persons will like. The situation is akin to sifting through data from sales reps concerning their customers.

The discussion usually begins with the assumption that the persons in question are male. That can be challenged immediately, for there is no overt evidence to support that conclusion. Also, another booby trap has been included. The two individuals are, in actuality, the same person! One of the offices described is at work, the other at home. The intent is to show the need to corroborate one's observations and not judge from a single incident or sample of one, even for the same person.

ASSIGNMENT 10a

OBSERVATION EXERCISE
An Office Visit

You have been provided the following descriptors on 2 individuals. Your task is to determine from this data how appropriate it would be to sell certain products to these persons. Write a short explanation for why you feel the person would desire your product and what type would be appropriate. Be fairly detailed about the type of product that is best, if any seems appropriate. Also, you should consider such details as the amount of product that would be consumed and even where that consumption might take place.

Example: Person A would be an ideal candidate for an expensive, manually operated 35mm camera that allows them to produce their own pictures and not be limited by a "do-all" that is completely automatic. Also, based on the products visible in their office, they appear to be less price sensitive and would buy a more expensive camera. Impressing associates with a fine camera might also be a factor.

Person B seems to be very practical and would like a fully automatic camera that doesn't get in the way. They might not even care about a camera at all but would just buy postcards or slides to avoid the hassle. Probably doesn't care what people think about the camera he carries.

Products		
restaurant	games	vehicle
hunting/fishing trip	sports club membership	computer
	TV/VCR	

Fortune
Wall Street Journal
7 Secrets of Successful People
Guerrilla Marketing
Smithsonian
Natural History

Robert Ludlum hardbacks (intrigue & spy novels)
Tom Clancy hardbacks

Roget's Thesaurus (hardback)

glass & steel desk
black marble desk accessories
gold ballpoint pen

stereo system tuned to classical music station

interesting artwork framed and adorning walls
       oil painting entitled "The Bookworm"
       art print by Durer, "Knight, Death and the Devil"

PERSON B

Reader's Digest
Guns & Ammo

local newspaper

Time-Life World War II series
Conan short stories (sword & sorcery paperbacks)

paperback dictionary

plastic desk organizers

plastic Papermate pens

clock-radio tuned to oldies station

framed posters on the walls
       Frazetta (artist for Conan books)
       Nagel

Discussion suggestions

Restaurants:

Person A: probably more interested in foreign foods than B as indicated by more "cultured" tastes in furniture and reading material. Foreign foods tend to require one to be somewhat adventuresome, unless you consider Taco Tico foreign food. Dining at an Ethiopian or Afghan restaurant might give one pause.

One should also ask how often these people tend to eat out and how much they would spend on an evening out. Person A would be a logical choice for more frequent dining out and at more expensive restaurants. Wine with dinner and an expensive dessert are not out of the question. The reason? The apparently higher disposable income for A.

Some students might infer that A would prefer to eat at home because they have refined cooking skills. Give them kudos for creativity.

What kinds of restaurants would A eat in besides foreign? Ones with a cocktail lounge and fine foods. More formal attire perhaps. For a quick meal? Quiche.

What reasons underlie eating out? Pleasure is a big one. Perhaps to experience something new or impress a client.

Person B: Here is a steak house person--Steak 'n Ale, Black Angus. McDonalds is OK for a quick bite (I prefer Burger King--juicier creations).

Foreign food? Probably Chinese/American or Mexican--foods so modified for American tastes that they really aren't foreign any longer. Might even think pizza is an Italian mainstay. Wouldn't touch escargot.

Doesn't eat out much except when traveling or on a date. Would not like to spend $100 on oneself for an evening out.

Games

In the past, we have focused on court sports--handball, squash, tennis and racquetball. Using that as a basis, one might find the following.

One should remember to ask the students why they reached the conclusions they did. The expression of wealth would lead to country clubs and eschewing the public courts, for example, as well as the fact that a "sedentary" lifestyle for a business executive demands some physical activity to offset stress and the high calories of fine food--or merely eating out because time does not permit cooking.

Person A:

Handball definitely. Likes to stay fit. Racquet sport choice would be squash (if he is very well off financially), tennis otherwise, but only at an exclusive club, not on public courts.

Other sports choices? saltwater fishing
                                    fly fishing
                                    golf (country club member)
                                    rowing

Person B:

Court sport would be racquetball.

Other sports choices: rugby

                                    bowling (too blue collar in this person's opinion)
                                    softball (not active enough)

Health club membership

Person A:

Nice gym with sauna, masseur, modern machines and aerobic equipment, tanning beds.

Person B:

Gold's Gym--dark sweatshop with free weights only. Torn muscle shirts. Lots of grunting and serious bodybuilders.

Guided hunting or fishing trip

Person A:

Where would they like their trip? Perhaps an exotic location like Africa or the Caribbean. Saltwater fishing is a definite possibility.

Game could include birds (in Spain or South America), sport fish (bonefish in Florida, trout in Montana, marlin in Baja), or big game (Cape buffalo, lion)

Person B:

It is suggested that this person would not really care about such an outing--they would be more likely to set up their own trip and forego a guide.

In general, one should consider usage rates as well as the absolute cost involved and the length of the trip.

Computer

Person A:

Students will undoubtedly begin naming brands at once, along with software options. Try to get them to focus first on whether the person would want a Mac, an IBM compatible or both. The graphics superiority of the former might be more appealing.

Styling? Maybe a NeXT would be attractive to this individual.

Also, how many computers would this person be in line for? One should not exclude the possibility that full size machines for the home and office would be appropriate, supplemented by a laptop for travel.

Person B:

Does this person even care about a computer? Would they use it for more than just video games?

TV & VCR

Person A: This person probably has a TV and VCR--virtually everyone does. Would it be a small portable or a nicer, larger one? Would it be a console model--one that looks like furniture, or something that is only a TV? What features on the VCR would you stress?

Person B: Definitely a console person here. Also a candidate for more than one TV. B probably watches more TV than A does and would use the VCR to either watch movies or tape shows that they would miss for other reasons--like watching another channel at the same time.

Vehicle

Person A: More than one car would be appropriate, if this person really has money. A sports car seems an obvious choice, as well as a nice "business" car like a BMW or perhaps a Mercedes.

Person B: Again, depending on the perception of wealth, one may imply that several vehicles might be suitable. In this case, the second vehicle chosen should be a pick-up truck or sport utility vehicle. Primary transportation would be more pedestrian. Maybe a Taurus. Which of the two would you choose to own a foreign car vs domestic?

OBSERVATION EXERCISE 2

ASSIGNMENT 10b. A Shopping Trip

This exercise is a field experience. You will be sent out to look at various malls or shopping areas in the city and asked to describe the character of the area and the type of people who shop there. Alternatively, if there are not malls or multiple shopping areas, you will be assigned to do the same for different types of stores that carry the same products. For example, the patrons of K-Mart (a discount retailer), J.C. Penney (a mid-range soft goods retailer) and The Bon Marche (a slightly upscale department store) could be compared.

When conducting your study, you should note such characteristics as:

Age of the shoppers

General attire

Number of children with shoppers

Types of cars most often seen (foreign/domestic; age; appearance)

Stores in the mall/shopping area besides "anchor" stores like Penney's or Nordstrom's--what are they like? what do they sell?

What other characteristics are seen? Is there a food plaza in the mall? What is it like?

Module 6

MATCHING DATA GATHERING METHODS AND RESPONDENTS

The severe budget constraints prevalent in today's business climate demand that the researcher be able to determine the most appropriate data collection method. Also, as others have pointed out, it is the quality of the data that is more important than the sample size. Hence, you will be asked to decide how to get the most rich information from the groups shown.

ASSIGNMENT 11

The following is a list of various groups and potential research topics. For each group, decide whether personal interview, telephone interview, or mail interview would be the most effective data collection method. State your reasons for each choice.

1. First Grade teachers in 5 local school districts. Effectiveness of a new learning tool.

Data collection mode:

> personal interview to introduce the product

> follow-up phone or mail survey

Reasons for use:

> In order to properly assess the quality and effectiveness of the new product, the teachers must be familiar with its use. After the test period, opinions can easily be collected by mail or phone.

2. Television viewers in your city. Opinions on a new local television news show.

Data collection mode:

> telephone interview

Reasons:

> Telephone technology makes it easy to dial random numbers. Non-viewers of the program can be screened out at the beginning of the interview.

3. Voters nationwide one day before a senate vote on a new tax on tobacco products.

Data collection mode:

telephone interview

Reasons:

Telephone interviews can be conducted quickly and easily. Centrally located telephone banks and Wide Area Telephone Service (WATS) can be used to randomly survey voters in various areas of the country. Results can be evaluated overnight and be ready for the morning news.

4. Patrons of a major hardware store chain. Preferences in tool brands.

Data collection mode:

personal interview

Reasons:

Personal interviews conducted during or after checkout would ensure that interviewees are actual patrons of the store chain, something which cannot be ascertained when randomly selecting their names from a directory. More detailed questions can be asked in the store as well, when the patron has the array of tools in front of them.

5. Movie patrons--taste preferences between air-popped and oil-popped popcorn.

Data collection mode:

personal interview

Reasons:

This will give the interviewers the opportunity to administer a taste test. It will also ensure that individuals surveyed have recently attended a movie screening. Their behavior or preferences at home may not necessarily correspond to how they act in a theater.

6. Travel agents in the larger cities in your home state. Changes in vacation trends.

Data collection mode:

Mail interview

Reasons:

Due to the often hectic working conditions present in travel agencies, telephone or personal interviews would not be effective or appreciated. Mail surveys could be completed over a period of time and with input from other agents within the business to get a more comprehensive response.

7. AARP members. Quality of services for the elderly.

Data collection mode:

mail interview or phone interview

Reasons:

Both methods have advantages and disadvantages. Some elderly have problems reading
and comprehending written surveys or may have trouble completing surveys due to illness.
On the other hand, telephone interviews may not be effective if the respondents have
difficulties hearing/understanding questions. Also, many elderly are suspicious of
telephone interviewers. A combination of both methods may provide the best results.
Phone numbers and addresses are easily available from the association.

8. Teenagers. Preferred athletic shoe brands.

Data collection mode:

personal interview

Reasons:

Teenagers are not very interested in completing mail surveys. It would be easier to
approach them in person either at school, youth centers or local shopping malls. One
would also tend to reduce the incidence of non-serious answers that might be prevalent on
mail surveys.

9. Shoppers in a local grocery store. Use of coupons.

Data collection mode:

observation

Reasons:

Observation would perhaps be best here. One could distribute the coupons in the store to interested patrons (perhaps at a display kiosk or on the shelf near the product) and then watch to see who takes them and who redeems them.

Module 7

QUESTIONNAIRE DESIGN

Students get far too little practice dealing with questionnaire design and correction. It is as much art as science, and requires some creative thinking. Two exercises are presented here. The first asks you to repair a set of random questions selected from several questionnaires. All are poorly worded or misleading--there are no trick questions that have no problems associated with them. The second exercise is a complete questionnaire that has numerous flaws and may require rewriting. Placement of questions, question design, sufficient number of questions for a given topic area, and category overlaps will all be included in this exercise.

Your first attempt at questionnaire design is often difficult and not very successful. Students in most principles of marketing classes may never learn to design questionnaires because they are running a simulation that does not require them to learn the basics of marketing research before they begin making marketing mix decisions. Hence, these exercises are designed to help you identify problems with survey instruments so that you can critique your own efforts prior to bringing them to the professor. It will also enable you to later understand how and why research by your own or other companies can be misleading and must be checked from the data gathering stage first.

ASSIGNMENT 12

Random Question Sheet

1. Do you have soda with your mixed drinks?   yes   no

2. Do you usually have beef or chicken at dinner?   yes   no

3. How much do you usually pay for a dozen eggs?

   a. less than 75 cents
   b. $.75 to $1.00
   c. $1.00 to $1.15
   d. $1.15 to $1.25
   e. over $1.25

4. Do you prefer large, inefficient engines in your car?

   yes   no

5. Is a transverse mounted engine something you would like in your next car?

   yes   no

6. Are you still beating your wife?

7. How long has it been since you last had a drink?

   a. today
   b. yesterday
   c. 2-4 days ago
   d. more than 5 days ago

8. How much alcohol do you drink in a month?
   a. none
   b. 1-4 cans of beer
   c. 5-12 cans of beer
   d. 13-24 cans of beer
   e. more than a case of beer

9. How likely is it that you would go to Greece on your next vacation?

   1   2   3   4   5   6
not at all   very
 likely   likely

70

10. What kind of car would you like to purchase next?
    a. sports car
    b. sedan
    c. station wagon
    d. utility vehicle

Proposed issues to consider with each question.

Question 1.

The question presumes you drink. This in itself may induce bias.

No frequency is asked. Alone, data are insufficient to make any meaningful decisions.

Yes/no answers are not very good, because if I _ever_ have soda with a drink I can say yes. Thus I may skew the results to appear more positive than reality. Note that the Simmons Data in a previous assignment sets the definition of "user" as someone who has consumed the product within the last 7 days.

What does soda mean? Club soda or soda pop? This is an example of a regional definition problem--soda is a common term for soft drinks east of the Mississippi, while west of the river people tend to use the term pop.

Question 2.

You can't answer an "or" question (Do you like A or B?) with a yes/no response.

Are those meats my only choices? What about pork, lamb or fish?

How would a vegetarian answer a dichotomous question like this?

What is dinner? The noon meal or the evening meal? Some people eat breakfast, lunch and dinner while others have breakfast, dinner and supper. The answers given may vary widely depending on which meal you think you are referring to and will be open to bias depending on whether the researcher identifies the meal in the same manner as the respondent.

What if I am a foreign family and I serve several meat entrees? It is not uncommon for Asians to have more than one meat dish at the table for a single meal.

Question 3.

There are price overlaps. For example, how would someone respond who believes they pay $1.00 for eggs--b or c?

Doesn't specify the color of the eggs--brown are more expensive than white. It only <u>assumes</u> we are speaking of white eggs.

Doesn't specify the size--, again an assumption is made that everyone will know we mean Grade A large.

It <u>does</u> specify one dozen--one thing done right, at least.

Question 4.

An example of a leading question. How can I answer yes to this? The results will be useless except for propaganda--they cannot be characterized as research.

Question 5.

This assumes the customer knows what the engine is. Most answers will be uninformed and therefore of limited value.

Question 6.

No answer possible that won't get the respondent in trouble.
Foreign respondents may not have the same social mores as Americans, however, and should be looked at as a subgroup within the larger sample.

Question 7.

A drink of what? Water? Everyone "knows" this question means a drink of some alcoholic beverage, don't they? Drive home the point that, insofar as possible, nothing should be open to question. Be specific in your question structure.

If the audience is alcoholic, they probably won't answer truthfully. If they are teenagers, they may inflate the answer to look more socially acceptable.

It may be that the respondent truly can't remember the answer, which means that we must screen our respondents carefully first.

No "e" for don't drink.

This answer is potentially biased greatly by the time of week or season when the question was asked. If you asked around New Years, almost everyone would answer the same way. Other times of the year the responses would be much different.

Also, if you asked people on Saturday, you would probably get an inordinate number of responses for "yesterday" because Friday night is a big drinking night. Care must be taken to spread out the timing of sampling to avoid this problem.

Question 8.

Gaps aren't consistent. There is really no reason to have the top category so wide and the earlier ones narrow in terms of number of cans drunk.

What about those who drink wine coolers or hard liquor? You don't have a translation factor from cans of beer to those other types of alcohol. There is no definition about the amount of alcohol in a can of beer. There is also a problem in that some people may drink bottles of beer and some may drink unusual size containers. For example, Foster's and Sapporo both come in cans that are far larger than 12 oz.

Youth may lie to be socially acceptable. Adults may understate for the same reason.

How the devil do I know how much I drink in a whole month?!? Give me a shorter time period. (Can you remember how much you drank in a single evening? Especially if you are drinking pitchers?)

Question 9.

This question is one which asks for speculation on the part of the respondent in may cases. You are likely to get an answer of "Who knows? I don't know anything about Greece." Besides, with the anti-American riots there during Bush's visit, I probably won't ever go there.

Question 10.

Who is the car for? The ultimate user of the vehicle will have a tremendous effect on my choice behavior. If it's for my teenager, none of the choices. They will get a subcompact with a wind-up engine and low insurance. If it's for my wife, she gets something higher off the ground for visibility and crash-worthiness. For me? I want a Dodge Stealth.

This is a forced choice question and should not be. Choices not exhaustive--no minivans, no compacts, no trucks.

New car or used? (need another question or series of them)

For many people, several options would fit. It depends on the price and lots of other factors not mentioned.

Define what you mean by "sports car", "sedan", "utility vehicle". My ideas may be different than yours. Some people may think a Geo Storm is a sports car rather than a subcompact.

ASSIGNMENT 13

Questionnaire Design

An inventor has designed a new product that he feels has great sales potential among golfers. This item is a cooler sleeve that attaches to the side of one's golf bag and has a spring loaded plunger so that drinks are always at hand when one opens the cooler. He has no idea of how to determine whether his product will sell and has tried to put together a marketing research questionnaire on his own. A sample of the questionnaire follows.

Your job is to fix his efforts so that he can determine a marketing strategy for his product.

1. What is your age? _____

2. What is your sex? _____

3. What was your disposable income last year?

    a. less than $15,000

    b. between $15,001.00 and $23, 000.00

    c. $23,000 to $37,000

    d. over $37,001

4. How often do you play golf?_____

5. Do you drink when you play golf?   yes   no

6. Do you own a golf cart? yes   no

7. How many children are in your family?

    a. none
    b. 1-3
    c. 4 or more

8. What color would you like to have in a golf bag accessory?

    a. black

    b. blue

    c. dark green

9. Where do you play golf?

    a. public course

    b. country club

10. Would you buy a drink cooler for your golf bag?

    yes   no

11. What is your occupation?

    a. doctor

    b. lawyer

    c. blue collar

    d. student

    e. unemployed

    f. manager

Please give us your name and phone number so that we can call later with details about our product.

Obviously, this questionnaire is fraught with problems. It is not greatly modified from ones submitted to class as a first draft, however.

A more completely designed instrument follows this series of discussion topics.

1. There is no introductory paragraph explaining what the research is for or who is conducting it.

2. The instrument has not been well designed for coding at all.

3. Students commonly put demographic information first, even after being told not to do so. It often leads to a non-response if placed first and in many cases isn't very useful information to have anyway. If the information is sought at the end of the questionnaire and not provided, at least the rest of the survey has been answered.

4. How important are age and sex? They perhaps play some role in the identification of what type of golfers might be displayed in advertising. Beyond that, they are just "nice to have".

5. Income categories belong at questionnaire's end. They are not consistent in their coverage-- they span from under $8000 in one instance to who knows what in the last.

Why include $1? It is not relevant for such large amounts, especially when people will be estimating.

Who knows what their **disposable** income is? How is that defined?

Ask students why income is included at all. They should know that a cross-tab between price for the product and preference to buy might be related to one's income.

The categories are not well chosen given current wages in the marketplace. The first category should be approximately $21,000 and under. People making less and still playing golf are probably students and would be identified with a cross-tab between occupation and income. Conversely, $37,000 as a top category is ridiculously low.

6. The question about golfing frequency should be prefaced with one at the very beginning of the survey asking if the respondent even plays golf. If they don't, they are not a likely candidate for the survey.

As with most questions, having categories for the respondent to fill out vastly improves the chances of a complete questionnaire. This one should not be open-ended. Also, it does not specify a time frame. How often per week? per season? per year?

7. Question 5 is loaded. It may result in an angry refusal from the respondent or just a blank. There are many ways to approach the central issue of the questionnaire more tactfully.

8. What is the purpose of question 6? There is no room on a golf cart for an ice chest, so using it as a platform for a portable refreshment stand is moot. It adds nothing to the issue and should be deleted.

9. Children? Does it matter?

10. Colors are nice, but the respondent doesn't know what we are trying to sell yet. Even if we showed them a model, the color choices aren't exhaustive. Moreover, we don't know to what degree they prefer one color over another. They might, given the instructions, circle them all, since we didn't specify circle only one. Even if they do indicate a single choice, we cannot know how intensely interested they are about it.

11. Does question 9 provide valuable information? Probably not. If placed early in the questionnaire, it could be used to get the individual involved without needing to think very hard about the response.

12. How can the respondent answer question 10 in an informed matter? They don't know anything about our product--price, materials it is constructed out of, capacity, quality--that would allow them to offer an opinion.

13. Occupations may be useful to know, but must be better categorized and include more options.

The following questionnaire represents a better attack on the problem. Note that it includes questions about the entire marketing mix--pricing, promotion, and distribution as well as product.

Hello, my name is _____ with CEMCO Market Research Associates. We are conducting a survey for a new product useful to golfers and would like your input. Your answers will remain strictly confidential and no salesman will call. The survey takes less than 5 minutes to complete. I need to ask you first if you play golf.

(If no, thank the person and go to the next respondent)

I. General Information

1. Where do you most often play golf? (circle only one)

    a. public courses

    b. country club courses

2. About how many times per year do you usually play golf?

    a. less than 6 times

    b. 6 to 12 times

    c. 13 to 24 times

    d. more than 24 times

3. Which months do you tend to play golf the most?
(circle only one)

    a. January through March

    b. April through June

    c. July through September

    d. October through December

4. When you play golf, do you have refreshments? (circle one)

    a. never

    b. only at the clubhouse

    c. a golf course employee brings them to me on the course

    d. I drink from the water fountains on the course

    e. other (please specify)

Our product is an insulated sleeve that attaches to your golf bag, allowing you to carry cold refreshments with you on the course. The sleeve is made of reinforced nylon and keeps your drinks cold for hours. There is a spring-loaded mechanism that pushes a fresh container to the top of the sleeve as each one is removed.

5. If you were to purchase such a product, in what color would you prefer it? Please rank your choices 1-5, with 1 being the most popular.

    _____ black

    _____ navy blue

    _____ teal

    _____ red

    _____ other (please specify)

6. What capacity would you like to see in your Cool-It?
    (circle one)

    a. 6 12 oz. cans

    b. 9 12 oz. cans

    c. 12 12 oz. cans

    d. other capacity (state your preference in number of 12 oz cans)

7. Assuming you would buy the 6 can size, what price would you feel comfortable paying for such an item? (circle one)

     a. less than $10.00

     b. $10.00 to $13.00

     c. $13.01 to $16.00

     d. $16.01 to $19.00

     e. over $19.00

8. If this product were available today at the price you were comfortable paying, how likely is it you would buy it the first time you saw it? (Circle one number)

1	2	3	4	5
not at all likely				very likely

8a. If you circled 2 or 1, please tell us why you are not interested.

9. If you were to buy this product, where would you go to purchase it? Please rank the following options, with 1 being the place you would shop at first to buy the product.

_____ sporting goods store (e.g. Big 5, SportWorld)

_____ golf specialty shops

_____ pro shops at courses

_____ general merchandise stores (e.g. Sears)

_____ other (please specify)

10. Which information sources do you use before you purchase golf equipment or accessories? Please rate **each** one as to its importance using the following scale:

1 = not at all important   2 = somewhat unimportant   3 = neutral
4 = somewhat important   5 = very important

club pro	1	2	3	4	5
golf magazines	1	2	3	4	5
salespeople	1	2	3	4	5
friends	1	2	3	4	5
TV					
ESPN	1	2	3	4	5
network sports programs	1	2	3	4	5
other (please specify)	1	2	3	4	5

II. Demographics

11. Gender (circle one)   male   female

12. Age on your last birthday:

      a. under 18
      b. 18 to 24
      c. 25 to 34
      d. 35 to 44
      e. 45 to 54
      f. over 55

13. Your occupation is (circle one please):

   a. professional (e.g. physician, lawyer)
   b. education
   c. skilled craftsman (e.g. carpenter, electrician)
   d. managerial
   e. clerical
   f. blue collar (e.g. assembly line worker)
   g. student
   h. homemaker
   i. retired
   j. other

14. Your approximate household income for 1993 was (circle one):

   a. under $20,000
   b. $20,000 to $35,000
   c. $35,000 to $55,000
   d. $55,000 to $75,000
   e. over $75,000

Comments:

THANK YOU FOR YOUR KIND ASSISTANCE!

ASSIGNMENT 14

Sample Size Problem

Based on a client's requirements of a confidence interval of 99 percent and acceptable sampling error of 2 percent, a sample size of 500 was calculated. The cost to the client would be $20,000. The client replies that the budget for this project is $17,000. What are the alternatives?

All students were able to come up with ideas about hiring college students to keep data collection costs down, and perhaps paring our fees as professional investigators. However, the latter cuts into the profits of the business. We pointed out the need to maintain a quality image for our company, as well as the fact that first class research costs money. It is, like in advertising, more important to ask the question first, then determine how much it will cost to achieve the goal, rather than set budgets and try to fit research designs to them.

Consequently, I asked my students to determine how much it cost per respondent to conduct the survey. This is only a rough calculation for illustrative purposes and does not, in a real life situation, often represent great cost savings because the additional cost of each individual survey is not merely the average of the overall project. Nonetheless, it was a place to start given the data at hand. Then I had them manipulate the confidence interval and acceptable sampling error to determine how many fewer people were needed to meet budget limitations. Holbert and Speece (Practical Marketing Research, 1993, Simon and Schuster) caution against adjusting confidence intervals because they are set by managers who presumably have a reason for selecting a given level, but there may be cases when the client is excessive in his/her demands for precision. I believe that students should be able to see how changes that will not interfere with meaningful results can be done, thus providing the client with the information they need and fulfilling one's obligation to one's employer.

Average cost per respondent is $40. (500 respondents divided by $20,000). If we assume that cost remains fixed, we can meet the client's budget with a sample of 425.

Now to the question of power. The approximate Z value for 99 percent confidence is 2.6, according to statistics tables in **Contemporary Marketing Research**, **2nd ed.**, McDaniel and Gates. The standard deviation in this problem is approximately 0.1720 (determined from original figures of sample size = 500, standard error of 2 percent and confidence interval of 99 percent.)

Calculating with sample size of 425, we hold standard deviation and sample error constant. Our Z value drops to roughly 2.3971. That is a confidence interval of over 98 percent. It is apparent that the sample size in this case can be manipulated with no loss of power.

ASSIGNMENT 15

Quota Sampling Exercise

As noted in your text, there are times when it is advisable or required that you do not do a random sample. This practice set will help you to see how a quota sample is drawn.

Your instructor will assign you a state capital to use as the basis for your quota sample. Your client is interested in finding out about the opinions of the people in the city but wants to be certain that certain groups are adequately represented in the sample. Your sample size is 600. The information can be found using the United States Census.

POPULATION FIGURES

1. The first step is to record the population figures for the groups in question. Your matrix will look as follows:

	Whites	Blacks	Hispanics	Row Total
18-24				
over 65				

Enter the population for each segment.

2. Now compute the proportion value for each cell. For example, divide the value in cell #1 by the total population of cells 1-6. Convert those numbers to percentages.

	Whites	Blacks	Hispanics	Row Total
18-24				
over 65				

3. Finally, determine the number of individuals in each cell by multiplying the percentages obtained in #2 by the sample size of 600.

	Whites	Blacks	Hispanics	Row Total
18-24				
over 65				

Module 9

DATA ANALYSIS

ASSIGNMENT 16

Dealing with Missing Data

In this exercise, you will be faced with a common problem--some of the respondents did not fill out their survey completely. Your job is 1) to determine whether or not to fill in the missing data 2) ascertain what impact is had by various approaches to dealing with missing data.

You have been asked to prepare a small sample of responses from young people concerning their reaction to mandatory national service. The dependent variable was a semantic differential with the following scale codes:

Not in 1   2   3   4   5   6   7   In favor
favor

You have been given a sample of 10 responses, the results of which are shown below. Demographic information is included with this data.

Person	Service	Age	Income
1	7	22	17,600
2	3	--	15,500
3	4	21	20,500
4	5	22	--
5	-	26	26,000
6	5	23	--
7	5	--	35,800
8	1	22	--
9	6	23	15,500
10	4	27	31,600

Compute the mean of each variable--service, age, income--using each of the following strategies to deal with the missing data.

1. Ignore missing data

service =

age   =

income =

2. Eliminate cases with missing data

service =

age   =

income =

3. Impute a value for missing data

(a) Random assignment

Use a random number table to select values to fill in the gaps in the table.

service =

age   =

income =

Explain how you arrived at the random income amount.

_____

_____

(b) Interpolate using a value from a similar case

service =

age   =

income =

(c) Insert the mean obtained from valid cases

service =

age   =

income =

4. Summary Table--Comparison of Missing Data Strategies

Technique	Means		
	Service	Age	Income
1. ignore missing values			
2. eliminate cases			
3a. impute random numbers			
3b. impute similar cases			
3c. impute mean			

Discuss your findings. What do you conclude?

_____

_____

_____

NOTES ON STATISTICS

We often referred to our numerical analysis classes as "sadistics". Actually, with a little work, the formulae and the output become familiar and are easy to work with. The problem lies in practicing with them until one understands what is useful when. The next page will provide an outline of what statistical tests are appropriate for which types of data.

It is most important that the student be able to take the computer printouts provided by the statistician and explain what they mean. Thus, the comprehensive case dealing with airline preference has been largely completed for you. You will be as to provide explanations as to what the data analysis means. You will be expected to be able to work with the statistics package on your own for the remaining cases, using the airlines case as your guide for commands and syntax for SPSS/PC+.

AREA OF APPLICATION	SUBGROUPS OR SAMPLES	LEVEL OF SCALING	TEST	SPECIAL REQUIREMENTS	EXAMPLE
Hypotheses about frequency distributions	One	Nominal	X^2	Random sample	Are observed differences in the numbers responding to three different promotions likely/not likely due to chance?
	Two or more	Nominal	X^2	Random sample, independent samples	Are differences in the numbers of men and women responding to a promotion likely/not likely due to chance?
	One	Ordinal	K–S	Random sample, natural order in data	Is the observed distribution of women preferring an ordered set of make-up colors (light to dark) likely/not likely due to chance?
Hypotheses about means	One (large sample)	Metric (interval or ratio)	Z-test for one mean	Random sample, $n \geq 30$	Is the observed difference between a sample estimate of the mean and some set standard or expected value of the mean likely/not likely due to chance?
	One (small sample)	Metric (interval or ratio)	t-test for one mean	Random sample, $n < 30$	Sample as for small sample
	Two (large sample)	Metric (interval or ratio)	Z-test for two means	Random sample, $n \geq 30$	Is the observed difference between the means for two subgroups (mean income for men and women) likely/not likely due to chance?
	Two (small sample)	Metric (interval or ratio)	One-way ANOVA	Random sample	Is the observed variation between means for three or more subgroups (mean expenditures on entertainment for high-moderate and low-income people) likely/not likely due to chance?
Hypotheses about proportions	One (large sample)	Metric (interval or ratio)	Z-test for one proportion	Random sample, $n \geq 30$	Is the observed difference between a sample estimate of proportion (percentage who say they will buy) and some set standard or expected value likely/not likely due to chance?
	Two (large sample)	Metric (interval or ratio)	Z-test for two proportions	Random sample, $n \geq 30$	Is the observed difference between estimated percentages for two subgroups (percentage of men and women who have college degrees) likely/not likely due to chance?

ASSIGNMENT 17a

Regression Basics

Regression analysis will allow you to determine whether a relationship between variables exists, as well as the direction and amount of change one can expect in one variable when other variables change.

The following situation concerns a company with national product sales. It has 20 regional distribution centers with roughly similar revenue generation. A new product is being test marketed in 10 regions, with differing levels of advertising in each. The table below shows the region, advertising expenditure and sales volume.

Region	Advertising ($ 000)	Sales ($ 000)
1	20	160
2	10	120
3	30	220
4	16	120
5	40	235
6	35	225
7	20	160
8	25	200
9	33	220
10	19	120

The regression equation is:

$$sales = 61.296 + 4.706 \text{ (advertising expenses)}$$

1. What is the predicted sales volume for an advertising budget of $22,000?

2. What is the predicted sales volume if we spend $80,000?

3. Do you see a problem with an $80,000 budget? Why or why not?

_____

_____

_____

4. Describe the implications of using your linear regression model if the advertising sales relationship looks like that illustrated below. Show graphically where the prediction error is.

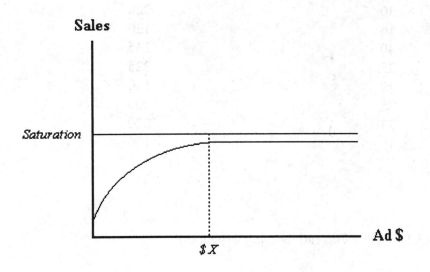

Module 10

SPSS PC+

The following is a brief introduction to the use of SPSS/PC+. For further information, please consult one of the excellent books on SPSS by Norusis. A suggested starter book is **The SPSS Guide to Data Analysis for SPSS/PC+**, 2nd edition.

How it works: a conceptual overview.

Data Input >>>>>>>>>>SPSS PROGRAM >>>>>>>>>>>>>>>>>> OUTPUT (results)
```
                     ^
                     ^
                     ^
             Instruction Input
```

Files:

Data input files:

FILE TYPE	COMMAND TO INPUT	CREATED BY
ASCII - Human readable files	Data List	WP or text editor
.WK1 - LOTUS 123 file	Translate from	Lotus123, Excel
.SPS - SPSS data file	GET	SPSS save Command
.SYS - SAME AS .sps " " " "	GET	SPSS save Command
.dbf - Dbase	Translate from	Dbase program

Program files:

ASCII only - Human readable-includes in Lower window of spss

F3 key in SPSS will allow input from files (make sure menu option is off)

Output files:

.Log - ASCII file with a list of all commands (instructions) that are run during the LAST session (does not include results)

.lis - ASCII file that includes output or results of running commands

Scratch.pad - last instruction set that was used (you should use the F9 key to save your program (instruction set) under a different name (prefer a:????.PRG)

Special Keys and their PRIMARY use:
F1 - lists files or variables located on disk
F2 - changes window structure
F3 - inserts files (I don't use this often)
F4 - Inserts lines (I don't use this often)
F5 - Looks up letters in the window (searches for specific letters)
F6 - Moves cursor
F7 - Marks an area or line for further use (same as F12 in WP)
F8 - Copy, Move or Delete lines marked by F7 command
F9 - SAVES INSTRUCTION SET -- **DO THIS OFTEN**
F10 - Runs instructions starting at cursor

alt-m - Toggles the menu on and off
alt-e - Moves the cursor from the menu to the lower window
alt-v - Shows you a list of the variables that can be used
alt-x - Allows for extended menu (more specific commands)

Windows
Menu - This allows you to write a program by choosing the appropriate command

Lower window - this includes the instruction set

Upper window - Shows the results of what has been run
(When menus are on part of this is hidden from view).

STATISTICS COMMANDS

The following example will walk you through the entire series of commands necessary to extract information from the case dealing with airline preference--Case B in the appendix of *Contemporary Marketing Research, 2nd ed.*, McDaniel and Gates.. You will be expected to handle the other cases on your own using this information as a guide.

NOTE: The punctuation marks in the lines of code are important. If you see a period or a space, it is there for a reason. Input the information EXACTLY as you see it to reduce the possibility of error.

First the data must be read into the program :

GET /FILE 'a:airline.sps'.

The file for the output should be clearly identified :

set /LISTING 'a:air_stat.out'.

Always run descriptive statistics to make sure the file is in proper order - there is no substitute for visual examination.

DESCRIPTIVES /VARIABLES ALL.

CHI SQUARED STATISTICS (command CROSSTABS)

NOTE: Chi-Squared statistics should NOT be run on variables with
high numbers of categories, nor should they be run on MANY
pairs of variables--this will create excessive output.

ALSO NOTE: you must include the STATISTICS= CHISQ command.

CROSSTABS /TABLES= Q1 BY Q12 Q10 Q9 Q8 /STATISTICS= CHISQ.

CROSSTABS /TABLES= Q2 BY Q12 Q10 Q9 Q8 /STATISTICS= CHISQ.

t-TESTS (tests for differences in means)

NOTE: t-tests REQUIRE at least interval data. In this (and most other) studies, Likert scales will be assumed interval. (the t-test command also provides correlation values and their significance).

t-tests between 2 different variables

T-TEST /PAIRS Q5A WITH Q5B Q5C Q5E Q5F.

t-tests on same variable between two different groups (e.g. male and female)

T-TEST /GROUPS Q12 (1,2) /VARIABLES Q5A Q5B Q5C Q5E Q5F.

ANOVA (Analysis of Variance)

ANOVA tests differences in variables with respect to several groups, unlike a t-test that only tests differences between two groups.

The next line of code will give the same results as the t-test (above) because it is only testing 2 variables.

ANOVA /VARIABLES Q5A Q5B Q5C Q5E Q5F BY Q12 (1,2).

The line of code below will examine the psychographic variables by education instead of gender.

ANOVA /VARIABLES Q5A Q5B Q5C Q5E Q5F BY Q8 (1,9).

ENTERING THE DATA INTO THE SPSS PROGRAM

Step 1: The Data List command pulls the data into the program. In this case, it is drawing it from the case files.

```
DATA LIST FILE 'a:airtravl.out' FIXED /id_num 1-4
job_num 5
q1 6
q2 7
q3a 8-9 q3b 10-11 q3c 12-13 q3d 14-15 q3e 16-17
q4a 18-19 q4b 20-21 q4c 22-23 q4d 24-25 q4e 26-27
q5 28 q5a 29 q5b 30 q5c 31 q5d 32 q5e 33 q5f 34 q5g 35 q5h 36 q5i 37 q5j 38
q5k 39 q5l 40 q5m 41 q5n 42 q5o 43
q6 44-45
q7 46-47
q8 48-49
q9 50
q10 51
q11 52-53
q12 54
trips 70-73
record 80.
```

Step 2: set /listing - tells the computer where to write an output file.

```
SET /LISTING 'a:airline.prt'.
```

Step 3: The Descriptives command shows various basic statistics of variables.

```
DESCRIPTIVES /VARIABLES ALL.
```

Step 4: The Frequencies command shows the distribution of the data.

NOTE: use frequencies command on only nominal or ordinal data.

```
FREQUENCIES /VARIABLES Q1 Q2 Q3A Q4A Q5A Q6 Q7 Q8 Q9 Q10 Q11 Q12.
```

Step 5: Variable Labels creates proper labels for the variables--this is done so that the variables can be easily identified later. Other people looking at your data may have no idea what FPOP means if you don't write out a label explaining it.

VARIABLE LABELS

Q1 'business trips'
Q2 'personal trips'
Q3A 'airline' Q3B 'airline' Q3C 'airline' Q3D 'airline'
Q3E 'airline'
Q4A 'leisure activity' Q4B 'leisure activity'
Q4C 'leisure activity' Q4D 'leisure activity'
Q4E 'leisure activity'
Q5A 'psychographic1' Q5B 'psychographic2' Q5C 'psychographic3'
Q5D 'psychographic4' Q5E 'psychographic5' Q5F 'psychographic6'
Q5G 'psychographic7' Q5H 'psychographic8' Q5I 'psychographic9'
Q5J 'psychographic10' Q5K 'psychographic11' Q5L psychographic12'
Q5M 'psychographic13' Q5N 'psychographic14' Q5O psychographic15'
Q6 'household size'
Q7 'age'
Q8 'education'
Q9 'employment'
Q10 'marital status'
Q11 'income level'
Q12 'gender'
TRIPS 'number of trips'.

Step 6: Value labels creates names for specific values of a variable so that the meaning of the numbers is easily interpreted.

NOTE: this is only used for nominal and ordinal variables.

VALUE LABELS Q1 to Q2 1 'one trip' 2 'two trips' 3 '3-4 trips' 4 '5-10 trips' 5 '11-25 trips' 6 '26 + trips' 7 'do not know' 8 'refused'
/Q3A to Q3E 1 'United' 2 'American' 3 'Delta' 4 'Continental' 5 'Midway' 6 'Northwest'
7 'US Air'
8 'Braniff' 9 'Pan Am' 10 'TWA' 11 'Mexicana' 12 'Eastern' 13 'Piedmont' 14 'other'
15 'refused'
/Q4A to Q4E 1 'hunting/fishing' 2 'team sports' 3 'jogging' 4 'swimming' 5 'camping'
6 'golf' 7 'workout' 8 'cycling' 9 'tennis' 10 'boating' 11 'bowling' 12 'waterski'
13 'snowski' 14 'read' 15 'TV' 16 'travel' 17 'movies' 18 'sewing' 19 'art/craft' 20 'shopping' 21
'music' 22 'sightseeing' 23 'sporting events' 24 'video' 25 'yardwork' 26 'socializing'
27 'children' 28 'organizations' 29 'house projects' 30 'decorating' 31 'other'
32 'do not know'
/Q5A to Q5O 1 'Strongly disagree' 2 'somewhat disagree' 3 'neutral' 4 'somewhat agree'
5 'strongly agree'
/Q6 9 '9 or more people' 10 'refused'

/Q7 1 '18-24' 2 '25-29' 3 '30-34' 4 '35-39' 5 '40-44' 6 '45-49' 7 '50-54' 8 '55-59' 9 '60-64'
10 '65 and over' 11 'refused'
/Q8 1 'grade school' 2 'some high school' 3 'HS grad' 4 'community college' 5 'vo-tech'
6 'college < 4yrs' 7 'college grad' 8 'some post-grad' 9 'grad degree' 10 'refused'
/Q9 1 'full-time' 2 'retired' 3 'part-time' 4 'homemaker' 5 'student' 6 'unemployed' 7 'refused'
/Q10 1 'married' 2 'single' 3 'divorced' 4 'widowed' 5 'refused'
/Q11 1 '< 10K' 2 '10-15K' 3 '15-20K' 4 '20-25K' 5 '25-30K'
6 '30-40K' 7 '40-50K' 8 '50-75K' 9 '75-100K' 10 '100-150K'
11 'over 150K' 12 'refused' 13 'refused < 40K' 14 'refused > 40K'
/Q12 1 'male' 2 'female'.

Step 7: Examine the difference in output between the descriptives command before and after
using variable and value labels.

DESCRIPTIVES /VARIABLES ALL.
FREQUENCIES /VARIABLES Q1 Q2 Q3A Q4A Q5A Q6 Q7 Q8 Q9 Q10 Q11 Q12.

Step 8: The SAVE command allows all changes to the data
to be saved in SPSS format.

SAVE /OUTFILE 'a:airline.sps'.

OUTPUT: AIRLINE PREFERENCE CASE

The following section is the output from SPSS/PC+ for the airline preference case.

Always run descriptive statistics to make sure the file is in proper order--there is no substitute for visual examination.

```
DESCRIPTIVES /VARIABLES ALL.
-------------------------------------------------------------------
```

Number of Valid Observations (Listwise) =   2.00

Variable	Mean	Std Dev	Minimum	Maximum	N	Label
ID_NUM	700.50	404.29	1	1400	1400	
JOB_NUM	2.00	.00	2	2	1400	
Q1	6.70	2.30	1	8	1400	
business	trips					
Q2	5.24	2.99	1	8	1400	
personal	trips					
Q3A	4.29	4.51	1	15	776	airline
Q3B	5.84	4.03	1	14	295	airline
Q3C	6.85	4.13	1	14	107	airline
Q3D	7.61	3.94	1	14	41	airline
Q3E	10.42	3.45	5	14	12	airline
Q4A	16.20	9.31	1	32	1400	leisure
activity						
Q4B	16.39	8.89	1	31	1034	leisure
activity						
Q4C	17.06	8.85	1	31	631	leisure
activity						
Q4D	17.63	8.76	1	31	339	leisure
activity						
Q4E	19.11	8.32	1	31	174	leisure
activity						
Q5	1.00	.00	1	1	1400	
Q5A	3.48	1.49	1	5	1400	
psychographic1						
Q5B	2.86	1.49	1	5	1400	
psychographic2						
Q5C	2.88	1.50	1	5	1400	
psychographic3						
Q5D	3.34	1.58	1	5	1400	
psychographic4						
Q5E	3.53	1.37	1	5	1400	
psychographic5						
Q5F	3.60	1.52	1	5	1400	
psychographic6						

Q5G psychographic7	2.61	1.46	1	5	1400	
Q5H psychographic8	3.68	1.42	1	5	1400	
Q5I psychographic9	3.12	1.51	1	5	1400	
Q5J psychographic10	2.55	1.60	1	5	1400	
Q5K psychographic11	3.01	1.53	1	5	1400	
Q5L psychographic12	3.66	1.34	1	5	1400	
Q5M psychographic13	1.83	1.26	1	5	1400	
Q5N psychographic14	3.42	1.34	1	5	1400	
Q5O psychographic15	2.72	1.43	1	5	1400	
Q6 household size	2.81	1.50	1	10	1400	
Q7	4.78	2.98	1	11	1400	age
Q8 education	5.26	2.20	1	10	1400	
Q9 employment	2.17	1.62	1	7	1400	
Q10 status	3.10	1.24	1	5	1400	marital
Q11 level	7.15	3.11	1	14	1400	income

Number of Valid Observations (Listwise) =   2.00

Variable	Mean	Std Dev	Minimum	Maximum	N	Label
Q12	1.52	.50	1	2	1400	gender
TRIPS	3.32	7.01	0	72	1400	number
of trips						
RECORD	1.00	.00	1	1	1400	

CHI SQUARED STATISTICS   (command CROSSTABS)

NOTE: Chi-Squared statistics should NOT be run on variables with high numbers of categories, nor should they be run on MANY pairs of variables--this will create excessive output.

ALSO NOTE: you must include the STATISTICS= CHISQ command.

CROSSTABS /TABLES= Q1 BY Q12 Q10 Q9 Q8 /STATISTICS= CHISQ.

Memory allows for 13,106 cells with 2 dimensions for general CROSSTABS.

(Some crosstabs are run here for illustration. They are not exhaustive, but do show some comparisons that are of interest to the researcher.)

Q1 business trips by Q12 gender

	Count	Q12 male	female	Row
		1	2	Total
Q1				
one trip	1	37	39	76 / 5.4
two trips	2	46	30	76 / 5.4
3-4 trips	3	47	19	66 / 4.7
5-10 trips	4	46	28	74 / 5.3
Column Total		666 / 47.6	734 / 52.4	1400 / 100.0

(Continued)

102

Q1 business trips by Q12 gender

```
                          Q12
             Count  ³
                    ³ male      female
                    ³                     Row
                    ³    1  ³       2  ³ Total
Q1          ÄÄÄÄÄÄÄÄÄÅÄÄÄÄÄÄÄÄÄÅÄÄÄÄÄÄÄÄÄ´
               5  ³     28  ³      5  ³    33
 11-25 trips      ³         ³         ³   2.4
                  ÄÄÄÄÄÄÄÄÄÄÅÄÄÄÄÄÄÄÄÄÄ´
               6  ³     22  ³      4  ³    26
 26 + trips       ³         ³         ³   1.9
                  ÄÄÄÄÄÄÄÄÄÄÅÄÄÄÄÄÄÄÄÄÄ´
               7  ³     21  ³     28  ³    49
 do not know      ³         ³         ³   3.5
                  ÄÄÄÄÄÄÄÄÄÄÅÄÄÄÄÄÄÄÄÄÄ´
               8  ³    419  ³    581  ³  1000
 refused          ³         ³         ³  71.4
                  ÄÄÄÄÄÄÄÄÄÄÁÄÄÄÄÄÄÄÄÄÄÙ
          Column      666       734      1400
          Total      47.6      52.4     100.0
```

Chi-Square	Value	DF	Significance
Pearson	72.28173	7	.00000
Likelihood Ratio	75.58678	7	.00000
Mantel-Haenszel test for linear association	31.22770	1	.00000

Minimum Expected Frequency -   12.369

Number of Missing Observations: 0

Q1 business trips by Q10 marital status

Q10

Count	married	single	divorced	widowed	refused	
	1	2	3	4	5	Row Total
Q1						
1 one trip	14	3	11	46	2	76 / 5.4
2 two trips	16	1	11	48		76 / 5.4
3 3-4 trips	13	2	12	39		66 / 4.7
4 5-10 trips	15		12	47		74 / 5.3
Column Total	305 / 21.8	84 / 6.0	184 / 13.1	819 / 58.5	8 / .6	1400 / 100.0

Q1 business trips by Q10 marital status

Q10

Count	married	single	divorced	widowed	refused	
	1	2	3	4	5	Row Total
Q1						
5 11-25 trips	5	6	7	20		33 / 2.4
6 26 + trips	2		1	23		26 / 1.9
7 do not know	11	1	7	30		49 / 3.5
8 refused	228	77	123	566	6	1000 / 71.4
Column Total	305 / 21.8	84 / 6.0	184 / 13.1	819 / 58.5	8 / .6	1400 / 100.0

Chi-Square	Value	DF	Significance
----------	-----	----	------------
Pearson	40.84038	28	.05554
Likelihood Ratio	50.15173	28	.00622
Mantel-Haenszel test for linear association	4.76982	1	.02896

Minimum Expected Frequency -   .149
Cells with Expected Frequency < 5 -   16 OF   40 (40.0%)

Number of Missing Observations: 0

Q1 business trips by Q9 employment

```
                    Q9
  Count  ³
       ³full-time retired  part-time homemaker student
            ³                                                Row
    ³        1  ³     2  ³     3  ³     4  ³     5  ³    Total
Q1   ÄÄÄÄÄÄÄÄÄÄÄÄÄÄÄÄÄÄÄÄÄÄÄÄÄÄÄÄÄÄÄÄÄÄÄÄÄÄÄÄÄÄÄÄÄÄÄÄÄÄÄÄÄÄÄÄÄÄ´
   1 ³    57  ³     9  ³        ³        ³     3  ³     76
 one trip    ³         ³        ³        ³        ³      5.4
     ÄÄÄÄÄÄÄÄÄÄÄÄÄÄÄÄÄÄÄÄÄÄÄÄÄÄÄÄÄÄÄÄÄÄÄÄÄÄÄÄÄÄÄÄÄÄÄÄÄÄÄÄÄÄÄÄÄÄ´
   2 ³    58  ³     7  ³     6  ³     2  ³        ³     76
 two trips   ³         ³        ³        ³        ³      5.4
     ÄÄÄÄÄÄÄÄÄÄÄÄÄÄÄÄÄÄÄÄÄÄÄÄÄÄÄÄÄÄÄÄÄÄÄÄÄÄÄÄÄÄÄÄÄÄÄÄÄÄÄÄÄÄÄÄÄÄ´
   3 ³    56  ³     4  ³        ³     4  ³     2  ³     66
 3-4 trips   ³         ³        ³        ³        ³      4.7
     ÄÄÄÄÄÄÄÄÄÄÄÄÄÄÄÄÄÄÄÄÄÄÄÄÄÄÄÄÄÄÄÄÄÄÄÄÄÄÄÄÄÄÄÄÄÄÄÄÄÄÄÄÄÄÄÄÄÄ´
   4 ³    58  ³    10  ³     2  ³     2  ³     2  ³     74
 5-10 trips  ³         ³        ³        ³        ³      5.3
     ÄÄÄÄÄÄÄÄÄÄÄÄÄÄÄÄÄÄÄÄÄÄÄÄÄÄÄÄÄÄÄÄÄÄÄÄÄÄÄÄÄÄÄÄÄÄÄÄÄÄÄÄÄÄÄÄÄÄÙ
Column    795      158     151      63     181     1400
Total     56.8     11.3    10.8     4.5     12.9    100.0
```

Q1 business trips by Q9 employment

	Q9		
Count	unemployed	refused	
	6	7	Row Total
Q1			
1 one trip	5	2	76 / 5.4
2 two trips	3		76 / 5.4
3 3-4 trips			66 / 4.7
4 5-10 trips			74 / 5.3
Column Total	46 / 3.3	6 / .4	1400 / 100.0

(Continued)

Q1 business trips by Q9 employment

	Q9					
Count	full-time	retired	part-time	homemaker	student	
	1	2	3	4	5	Row Total
Q1						
5 11-25 trips	28	4			1	33 / 2.4
6 26 + trips	21	2	2		1	26 / 1.9
7 do not know	22	8	8	3	6	49 / 3.5
8 refused	495	114	133	52	166	1000 / 71.4
Column Total	795 / 56.8	158 / 11.3	151 / 10.8	63 / 4.5	181 / 12.9	1400 / 100.0

Q1 business trips by Q9 employment

```
                     Q9
         Count   ³
                 ³ unemployed refused
                 ³                        Row
                 ³     6    ³     7  ³  Total
Q1       ÄÄÄÄÄÄÄÄÄÄÅÄÄÄÄÄÄÄÄÄÄÄÅÄÄÄÄÄÄÄÄÄÄÄ´
              5   ³          ³        ³    33
  11-25 trips     ³          ³        ³   2.4
                 ÄÄÄÄÄÄÄÄÄÄÄÄÅÄÄÄÄÄÄÄÄÄÄÄ´
              6   ³          ³        ³    26
  26 + trips      ³          ³        ³   1.9
                 ÄÄÄÄÄÄÄÄÄÄÄÄÅÄÄÄÄÄÄÄÄÄÄÄ´
              7   ³     2    ³        ³    49
  do not know     ³          ³        ³   3.5
                 ÄÄÄÄÄÄÄÄÄÄÄÄÅÄÄÄÄÄÄÄÄÄÄÄ´
              8   ³    36    ³     4  ³  1000
  refused         ³          ³        ³  71.4
                 ÄÄÄÄÄÄÄÄÄÄÄÄÄÄÄÄÄÄÄÄÄÄÄÄÙ
         Column      46           6      1400
         Total      3.3          .4     100.0
```

Chi-Square	Value	DF	Significance
Pearson	146.29368	42	.00000
Likelihood Ratio	190.11227	42	.00000
Mantel-Haenszel test for linear association	66.34078	1	.00000

Minimum Expected Frequency -   .111
Cells with Expected Frequency < 5 -   28 OF   56 (50.0%)

Number of Missing Observations: 0

Q1 business trips by Q8 education

Q8

```
Count    │
         │grade   some high   high school  community  vo-tech
         │school  school      graduate     college
                                                              Row
         │      1 │      2 │       3 │        4 │       5 │Total
Q1       ÄÄÄÄÄÄÄÄÄÅÄÄÄÄÄÄÄÄÄÅÄÄÄÄÄÄÄÄÄÅÄÄÄÄÄÄÄÄÄÄÅÄÄÄÄÄÄÄÄÄÄÄÄÄ
 1       │        │      4 │      18 │        5 │       2 │ 76
  one trip│        │        │         │          │         │ 5.4
         ÄÄÄÄÄÄÄÄÄÅÄÄÄÄÄÄÄÄÄÅÄÄÄÄÄÄÄÄÄÅÄÄÄÄÄÄÄÄÄÄÅÄÄÄÄÄÄÄÄÄÄÄÄÄ
 2       │        │      2 │       8 │        6 │       4 │ 76
  two trips│        │        │         │          │         │ 5.4
         ÄÄÄÄÄÄÄÄÄÅÄÄÄÄÄÄÄÄÄÅÄÄÄÄÄÄÄÄÄÅÄÄÄÄÄÄÄÄÄÄÅÄÄÄÄÄÄÄÄÄÄÄÄÄ
 3       │        │      2 │       4 │        2 │       1 │ 66
  3-4 trips│        │        │         │          │         │ 4.7
         ÄÄÄÄÄÄÄÄÄÅÄÄÄÄÄÄÄÄÄÅÄÄÄÄÄÄÄÄÄÅÄÄÄÄÄÄÄÄÄÄÅÄÄÄÄÄÄÄÄÄÄÄÄÄ
 4       │        │        │      11 │          │       6 │ 74
  5-10 trips│        │        │         │          │         │ 5.3
         ÄÄÄÄÄÄÄÄÄÅÄÄÄÄÄÄÄÄÄÅÄÄÄÄÄÄÄÄÄÅÄÄÄÄÄÄÄÄÄÄÅÄÄÄÄÄÄÄÄÄÄÄÄÙ
Column      20       110        354         70         57   1400
 Total     1.4       7.9       25.3        5.0        4.1  100.0
```

Q1 business trips by Q8 education

Q8

```
Count     ³
          ³ college    college      some         grad       refused
          ³ < 4yrs     grad         post-grad    degree
                                                                      Row
          ³     6   ³     7    ³      8     ³      9    ³    10    Total
Q1         ÄÄÄÄÄÄÄÄÄÄÅÄÄÄÄÄÄÄÄÄÄÅÄÄÄÄÄÄÄÄÄÄÅÄÄÄÄÄÄÄÄÄÄÅÄÄÄÄÄÄÄÄÄÄ´
  1    ³  15    ³    24   ³      3     ³      5    ³         ³  76
  one trip      ³         ³            ³           ³         ³  5.4
           ÄÄÄÄÄÄÄÄÄÄÅÄÄÄÄÄÄÄÄÄÄÅÄÄÄÄÄÄÄÄÄÄÅÄÄÄÄÄÄÄÄÄÄÅÄÄÄÄÄÄÄÄÄÄ´
  2    ³  11    ³    23   ³      3   ³     19    ³         ³  76
  two trips     ³         ³            ³           ³         ³  5.4
           ÄÄÄÄÄÄÄÄÄÄÅÄÄÄÄÄÄÄÄÄÄÅÄÄÄÄÄÄÄÄÄÄÅÄÄÄÄÄÄÄÄÄÄÅÄÄÄÄÄÄÄÄÄÄ´
  3    ³  15    ³    22   ³      7   ³     11   ³    2   ³  66
  3-4 trips     ³         ³            ³           ³         ³  4.7
           ÄÄÄÄÄÄÄÄÄÄÅÄÄÄÄÄÄÄÄÄÄÅÄÄÄÄÄÄÄÄÄÄÅÄÄÄÄÄÄÄÄÄÄÅÄÄÄÄÄÄÄÄÄÄ´
  4    ³  18    ³    24   ³      1   ³     14   ³         ³  74
  5-10 trips    ³         ³            ³           ³         ³  5.3
           ÄÄÄÄÄÄÄÄÄÄÅÄÄÄÄÄÄÄÄÄÄÅÄÄÄÄÄÄÄÄÄÄÅÄÄÄÄÄÄÄÄÄÄÅÄÄÄÄÄÄÄÄÄÄÙ
Column     355          252          46         123          13     1400
Total      25.4        18.0         3.3         8.8          .9     100.0
```

Q1 business trips by Q8 education

Q8

Count	grade school	some high school	high school graduate	community college	vo-tech	Row Total
	1	2	3	4	5	
Q1						
5 11-25 trips			6			33 2.4
6 26 + trips			1			26 1.9
7 do not know		1	18	1	2	49 3.5
8 refused	20	101	288	56	42	1000 71.4
Column Total	20 1.4	110 7.9	354 25.3	70 5.0	57 4.1	1400 100.0

110

Q1 business trips by Q8 education

Q8

Count	college < 4yrs	college grad	some post-grad	grad degree	refused	Row Total
Q1	6	7	8	9	10	
5 11-25 trips	4	14	2	7		33 2.4
6 26 + trips	5	8	3	9		26 1.9
7 do not know	12	8	3	3	1	49 3.5
8 refused	275	129	24	55	10	1000 71.4
Column Total	355 25.4	252 18.0	46 3.3	123 8.8	13 .9	1400 100.0

Chi-Square	Value	DF	Significance
Pearson	253.07349	63	.00000
Likelihood Ratio	258.43322	63	.00000
Mantel-Haenszel test for linear association	89.42575	1	.00000

Minimum Expected Frequency -   .241
Cells with Expected Frequency < 5 -   42 OF   80 (52.5%)

Number of Missing Observations: 0

111

CROSSTABS /TABLES= Q2 BY Q12 Q10 Q9 Q8 /STATISTICS= CHISQ.

Memory allows for 13,106 cells with 2 dimensions for general CROSSTABS.

Q2 personal trips by Q12 gender

Q2	Count	Q12 male 1	female 2	Row Total
one trip	1	113	127	240 17.1
two trips	2	76	95	171 12.2
3-4 trips	3	76	74	150 10.7
5-10 trips	4	47	35	82 5.9
Column Total		666 47.6	734 52.4	1400 100.0

(Continued)

Q2 personal trips by Q12 gender

Q2	Count	Q12 male 1	female 2	Row Total
11-25 trips	5	8	7	15 1.1
26 + trips	6		3	3 .2
do not know	7	12	13	25 1.8
refused	8	334	380	714 51.0
Column Total		666 47.6	734 52.4	1400 100.0

112

Chi-Square	Value	DF	Significance
Pearson	7.49562	7	.37916
Likelihood Ratio	8.64876	7	.27887
Mantel-Haenszel test for linear association	.06963	1	.79188

Minimum Expected Frequency -   1.427
Cells with Expected Frequency < 5 -   2 OF   16 (12.5%)

Number of Missing Observations: 0

Q2 personal trips by Q9 employment

                Q9

Count
       full-time retired part-time homemaker student

Q2	1	2	3	4	5	Row Total
1 one trip	139	23	28	17	24	240 / 17.1
2 two trips	108	16	17	9	16	171 / 12.2
3 3-4 trips	92	19	10	6	23	150 / 10.7
4 5-10 trips	48	14	6	6	6	82 / 5.9
Column Total	795 / 56.8	158 / 11.3	151 / 10.8	63 / 4.5	181 / 12.9	1400 / 100.0

113

Q2   personal trips   by   Q9   employment

```
                          Q9
              Count    ³
                       ³unemployed refused
                       ³                        Row
                       ³      6   ³      7   ³ Total
Q2            ÄÄÄÄÄÄÄÄÄÄÅÄÄÄÄÄÄÄÄÄÄÅÄÄÄÄÄÄÄÄÄÄ´
              1    ³      7   ³      2   ³   240
   one trip        ³          ³          ³   17.1
              ÄÄÄÄÄÄÄÄÄÄÅÄÄÄÄÄÄÄÄÄÄÅÄÄÄÄ´
              2    ³      3   ³      2   ³   171
   two trips       ³          ³          ³   12.2
              ÄÄÄÄÄÄÄÄÄÄÅÄÄÄÄÄÄÄÄÄÄÅÄÄÄÄ´
              3    ³          ³          ³   150
   3-4 trips       ³          ³          ³   10.7
              ÄÄÄÄÄÄÄÄÄÄÅÄÄÄÄÄÄÄÄÄÄÅÄÄÄÄ´
              4    ³      2   ³          ³    82
   5-10 trips      ³          ³          ³    5.9
              ÄÄÄÄÄÄÄÄÄÄÁÄÄÄÄÄÄÄÄÄÄÁÄÄÄÄÙ
              Column        46         6      1400
(Continued)   Total        3.3        .4     100.0
```

Q2   **personal trips   by   Q9   employment**

```
                          Q9

Count      ³
           ³full-time retired   part-time homemaker student
           ³                                                     Row
           ³    1   ³    2   ³    3   ³    4   ³    5   ³ Total
Q2         ÄÄÄÄÄÄÄÄÄÅÄÄÄÄÄÄÄÄÄÅÄÄÄÄÄÄÄÄÄÅÄÄÄÄÄÄÄÄÄÅÄÄÄÄÄÄÄÄÄ´
5    ³    11   ³    3   ³        ³        ³    1   ³    15
11-25 trips     ³        ³        ³        ³        ³    1.1
           ÄÄÄÄÄÄÄÄÄÅÄÄÄÄÄÄÄÄÄÅÄÄÄÄÄÄÄÄÄÅÄÄÄÄÄÄÄÄÄÅÄÄÄÄÄÄÄÄÄ´
6    ³     2   ³        ³    1   ³        ³        ³     3
26 + trips      ³        ³        ³        ³        ³    .2
           ÄÄÄÄÄÄÄÄÄÅÄÄÄÄÄÄÄÄÄÅÄÄÄÄÄÄÄÄÄÅÄÄÄÄÄÄÄÄÄÅÄÄÄÄÄÄÄÄÄ´
7    ³    13   ³    6   ³    1   ³        ³    4   ³    25
do not know     ³        ³        ³        ³        ³    1.8
           ÄÄÄÄÄÄÄÄÄÅÄÄÄÄÄÄÄÄÄÅÄÄÄÄÄÄÄÄÄÅÄÄÄÄÄÄÄÄÄÅÄÄÄÄÄÄÄÄÄ´
8    ³   382   ³   77   ³   88   ³   25   ³  107   ³   714
refused         ³        ³        ³        ³        ³   51.0
           ÄÄÄÄÄÄÄÄÄÁÄÄÄÄÄÄÄÄÄÁÄÄÄÄÄÄÄÄÄÁÄÄÄÄÄÄÄÄÄÁÄÄÄÄÄÄÄÄÄÙ
Column    795      158      151       63      181     1400
 Total    56.8     11.3     10.8      4.5     12.9    100.0
-----------------------------------------------------------
```

114

Q2 personal trips by Q9 employment

```
                         Q9
             Count  ³
                    ³ unemployed refused
                                            Row
                    ³    6    ³    7    ³   Total
Q2           ÄÄÄÄÄÄÄÄÄÅÄÄÄÄÄÄÄÄÄÅÄÄÄÄÄÄÄÄÄ´
                  5  ³         ³         ³    15
  11-25 trips       ³         ³         ³   1.1
             ÄÄÄÄÄÄÄÄÄÅÄÄÄÄÄÄÄÄÄÅÄÄÄÄÄÄÄÄÄ´
                  6  ³         ³         ³     3
  26 + trips        ³         ³         ³    .2
             ÄÄÄÄÄÄÄÄÄÅÄÄÄÄÄÄÄÄÄÅÄÄÄÄÄÄÄÄÄ´
                  7  ³    1    ³         ³    25
  do not know       ³         ³         ³   1.8
             ÄÄÄÄÄÄÄÄÄÅÄÄÄÄÄÄÄÄÄÅÄÄÄÄÄÄÄÄÄ´
                  8  ³    33   ³    2    ³   714
  refused           ³         ³         ³  51.0
             ÄÄÄÄÄÄÄÄÄÁÄÄÄÄÄÄÄÄÄÁÄÄÄÄÄÄÄÄÄÙ
             Column      46        6        1400
             Total       3.3       .4      100.0
```

Chi-Square	Value	DF	Significance
Pearson	56.01111	42	.07260
Likelihood Ratio	64.75834	42	.01361
Mantel-Haenszel test for linear association	7.28224	1	.00696

Minimum Expected Frequency -   .013
Cells with Expected Frequency < 5 -   27 OF   56 (48.2%)

Number of Missing Observations: 0

t-TESTS   (tests for differences in means)

NOTE: t-tests REQUIRE at least interval data--in this (and most other) studies, Likert scales will be assumed interval. The t-test command also provides correlation values and their significance.

* t-tests between 2 different variables *

T-TEST /PAIRS Q5A WITH Q5B Q5C Q5E Q5F.
T-TEST requires 256 BYTES of workspace for execution.

- - - t-tests for paired samples - - -

Variable	Number of pairs	Corr	2-tail Sig	Mean	SD	SE of Mean
Q5A psychographic1				3.4821	1.491	.040
	1400	.062	.021			
Q5B psychographic2				2.8550	1.492	.040

Paired Differences						
Mean	SD	SE of Mean	t-value	df	2-tail Sig
.6271	2.044	.055	11.48	1399	.000

95% CI (.520, .734)

- - - t-tests for paired samples - - -

Variable	Number of pairs	Corr	2-tail Sig	Mean	SD	SE of Mean
Q5A psychographic1				3.4821	1.491	.040
	1400	.079	.003			
Q5C psychographic3				2.8757	1.503	.040

Paired Differences						
Mean	SD	SE of Mean	t-value	df	2-tail Sig
.6064	2.032	.054	11.17	1399	.000

95% CI (.500, .713)

- - - t-tests for paired samples - - -

Variable	Number of pairs	Corr	2-tail Sig	Mean	SD	SE of Mean
Q5A psychographic1				3.4821	1.491	.040
	1400	.156	.000			
Q5E psychographic5				3.5300	1.373	.037

ÄÄ

Paired Differences [3]

Mean	SD	SE of Mean	[3]	t-value	df	2-tail Sig
-.0479	1.863	.050	[3]	-.96	1399	.337

95% CI (-.146, .050)   [3]

- - - t-tests for paired samples - - -

Variable	Number of pairs	Corr	2-tail Sig	Mean	SD	SE of Mean
Q5A psychographic1				3.4821	1.491	.040
	1400	.061	.022			
Q5F psychographic6				3.5971	1.523	.041

Paired Differences [3]

Mean	SD	SE of Mean	[3]	t-value	df	2-tail Sig
-.1150	2.065	.055	[3]	-2.08	1399	.037

95% CI (-.223, -.007)   [3]

* t-tests on same variable between two different groups (e.g. male and female) *

T-TEST /GROUPS Q12 (1,2) /VARIABLES Q5A Q5B Q5C Q5E Q5F.
T-TEST requires 360 BYTES of workspace for execution.

t-tests for independent samples of Q12   gender

Variable	Number of Cases	Mean	SD	SE of Mean

ÄÄ
Q5A   psychographic1

male	666	3.5195	1.505	.058
female	734	3.4482	1.479	.055

ÄÄ

Mean Difference = .0713

Levene's Test for Equality of Variances: F= .043

P= .835

t-test for Equality of Means

Variances	t-value	df	2-Tail Sig	SE of Diff	95% CI for Diff

ÄÄ

Equal	.89	1398	.372	.080	(-.085, .228)
Unequal	.89	1379.85	.372	.080	(-.085, .228)

ÄÄ
t-tests for independent samples of Q12   gender

Variable	Number of Cases	Mean	SD	SE of Mean

ÄÄ

Q5B   psychographic2

male	666	2.9294	1.528	.059
female	734	2.7875	1.457	.054

ÄÄ

Mean Difference = .1420

Levene's Test for Equality of Variances: F= 4.009

P= .045

t-test for Equality of Means

Variances	t-value	df	2-Tail Sig	SE of Diff	95% CI for Diff
Equal	1.78	1398	.075	.080	(-.015, .299)
Unequal	1.77	1369.54	.076	.080	(-.015, .299)

t-tests for independent samples of Q12   gender

Variable	Number of Cases	Mean	SD	SE of Mean

Q5C psychographic3

male	666	2.8213	1.452	.056
female	734	2.9251	1.546	.057

Mean Difference = -.1037

Levene's Test for Equality of Variances: F= 11.642
P= .001

t-test for Equality of Means

Variances	t-value	df	2-Tail Sig	SE of Diff	95% CI for Diff
Equal	-1.29	1398	.197	.080	(-.261, .054)
Unequal	-1.29	1396.37	.196	.080	(-.261, .054)

t-tests for independent samples of   Q12   gender

| | Number | | | |
|Variable | of Cases | Mean | SD | SE of Mean |

ÄÄ
Q5E   psychographic5

| male | 666 | 3.6967 | 1.336 | .052 |
| female | 734 | 3.3787 | 1.390 | .051 |

ÄÄ

Mean Difference = .3180

Levene's Test for Equality of Variances: F= 13.435
P= .000

t-test for Equality of Means

| | | | | | 95% |
| Variances | t-value | df | 2-Tail Sig | SE of Diff | CI for Diff |

ÄÄ
| Equal | 4.35 | 1398 | .000 | .073 | (.175, .461) |
| Unequal | 4.36 | 1393.40 | .000 | .073 | (.175, .461) |
ÄÄ
----

t-tests for independent samples of   Q12   gender

	Number			
Variable	of Cases	Mean	SD	SE of Mean
Q5F psychographic6				

| male | 666 | 3.2583 | 1.548 | .060 |
| female | 734 | 3.9046 | 1.433 | .053 |

Mean Difference = -.6464

Levene's Test for Equality of Variances: F= 31.859
P= .000

t-test for Equality of Means

| | | | | | 95% |
| Variances | t-value | df | 2-Tail Sig | SE of Diff | CI for Diff |

| Equal | -8.11 | 1398 | .000 | .080 | (-.803, -.490) |
| Unequal | -8.08 | 1356.93 | .000 | .080 | (-.803, -.489) |

ANOVA (Analysis of Variance)

Tests differences in variables with respect to several groups-- unlike t-test that only tests difference between two groups.

* This will give the same results as the t-test (above) *.
ANOVA /VARIABLES Q5A Q5B Q5C Q5E Q5F BY Q12 (1,2).

'ANOVA' PROBLEM REQUIRES   526 BYTES OF MEMORY.

* * * A N A L Y S I S   O F   V A R I A N C E * * *

```
        Q5A        psychographic1
   BY   Q12        gender
```

Source of Variation	Sum of Squares	DF	Mean Square	F	Signif of F
Main Effects	1.775	1	1.775	.798	.372
Q12	1.775	1	1.775	.798	.372
Explained	1.775	1	1.775	.798	.372
Residual	3109.779	1398	2.224		
Total	3111.554	1399	2.224		

1400 Cases were processed.
   0 Cases (.0 PCT) were missing.

* * * A N A L Y S I S   O F   V A R I A N C E * * *

```
        Q5B        psychographic2
   BY   Q12        gender
```

Source of Variation	Sum of Squares	DF	Mean Square	F	Signif of F
Main Effects	7.037	1	7.037	3.165	.075
Q12	7.037	1	7.037	3.165	.075
Explained	7.037	1	7.037	3.165	.075
Residual	3108.528	1398	2.224		
Total	3115.565	1399	2.227		

1400 Cases were processed.
0 Cases (.0 PCT) were missing.
* * * A N A L Y S I S   O F   V A R I A N C E * * *

        Q5C   psychographic3
    BY Q12   gender

Source of Variation	Sum of Squares	DF	Mean Square	F	Signif of F
Main Effects	3.758	1	3.758	1.666	.197
Q12	3.758	1	3.758	1.666	.197
Explained	3.758	1	3.758	1.666	.197
Residual	3154.616	1398	2.257		
Total	3158.374	1399	2.258		

1400 Cases were processed.
0 Cases (.0 PCT) were missing.

* * * A N A L Y S I S   O F   V A R I A N C E * * *

        Q5E   psychographic5
    BY Q12   gender

Source of Variation	Sum of Squares	DF	Mean Square	F	Signif of F
Main Effects	35.299	1	35.299	18.955	.000
Q12	35.299	1	35.299	18.955	.000
Explained	35.299	1	35.299	18.955	.000
Residual	2603.441	1398	1.862		
Total	2638.740	1399	1.886		

----

* * * A N A L Y S I S   O F   V A R I A N C E * * *

Q5F   psychographic6
BY   Q12   gender

Source of Variation	Sum of Squares	DF	Mean Square	F	Signif of F
Main Effects	145.885	1	145.885	65.813	.000
Q12	145.885	1	145.885	65.813	.000
Explained	145.885	1	145.885	65.813	.000
Residual	3098.904	1398	2.217		
Total	3244.789	1399	2.319		

1400 Cases were processed.
   0 Cases (.0 PCT) were missing.

* This will examine the psychographic variables by education instead of gender*.

ANOVA /VARIABLES Q5A Q5B Q5C Q5E Q5F BY Q8 (1,9).

'ANOVA' PROBLEM REQUIRES   2038 BYTES OF MEMORY.

* * * A N A L Y S I S   O F   V A R I A N C E * * *

	Q5A	psychographic1
BY	Q8	education

Source of Variation	Sum of Squares	DF	Mean Square	F	Signif of F
Main Effects	128.567	8	16.071	7.462	.000
Q8	128.567	8	16.071	7.462	.000
Explained	128.567	8	16.071	7.462	.000
Residual	2967.677	1378	2.154		
Total	3096.244	1386	2.234		

1400 Cases were processed.
13 Cases (.9 PCT) were missing.

* * * A N A L Y S I S   O F   V A R I A N C E * * *

	Q5B	psychographic2
BY	Q8	education

Source of Variation	Sum of Squares	DF	Mean Square	F	Signif of F
Main Effects	150.179	8	18.772	8.807	.000
Q8	150.179	8	18.772	8.807	.000
Explained	150.179	8	18.772	8.807	.000
Residual	2937.110	1378	2.131		
Total	3087.289	1386	2.227		

1400 Cases were processed.
13 Cases (.9 PCT) were missing.

```
            Q5C         psychographic3
      BY    Q8          education

Source of      Sum of                    Mean                 Signif
Variation      Squares       DF          Square       F       of F

Main Effects   40.115         8          5.014       2.248    .022
  Q8           40.115         8          5.014       2.248    .022

Explained      40.115         8          5.014       2.248    .022

Residual       3073.475     1378         2.230

Total          3113.590     1386         2.246
```

1400 Cases were processed. 13 Cases (.9 PCT) were missing.

```
            Q5E         psychographic5
      BY    Q8          education


Source of      Sum of                    Mean                 Signif
Variation      Squares       DF          Square       F       of F

Main Effects   27.021         8          3.378       1.791    .075
  Q8           27.021         8          3.378       1.791    .075

Explained      27.021         8          3.378       1.791    .075

Residual       2598.920     1378         1.886

Total          2625.941     1386         1.895
```

1400 Cases were processed. 13 Cases (.9 PCT) were missing.

```
            Q5F         psychographic6
      BY    Q8          education

Source of      Sum of                    Mean                 Signif
Variation      Squares       DF          Square       F       of F

Main Effects   50.980         8          6.373       2.761    .005
  Q8           50.980         8          6.373       2.761    .005

Explained      50.980         8          6.373       2.761    .005

Residual       3180.232     1378         2.308

Total          3231.213     1386         2.331
FINISH.
```